Communication for another development

Communication

for another development

Listening before telling

WENDY QUARRY AND RICARDO RAMÍREZ

Zed Books
LONDON & NEW YORK

Communication for Another Development: Listening before Telling was first published in 2009 by Zed Books Ltd, 7 Cynthia Street, London N1 9JF, UK and Room 400, 175 Fifth Avenue, New York, NY 10010, USA

www.zedbooks.co.uk

All chapter title page illustrations by Ricardo Ramírez
Planner gliding illustration on p. ii and in Chapter 3 by Rius (Eduardo del Río, Mexico)

Designed and typeset in Monotype Ehrhardt by illuminati, Grosmont, www.illuminatibooks.co.uk
Index by John Barker
Cover designed by Rogue Four Design
Printed and bound in Great Britain by CPI Antony Rowe, Chippenham and Eastbourne

Distributed in the USA exclusively by Palgrave Macmillan, a division of St Martin's Press, LLC, 175 Fifth Avenue, New York, NY 10010, USA

A catalogue record for this book is available from the British Library
Library of Congress Cataloging in Publication Data available

ISBN   978 1 84813 008 1 Hb
ISBN   978 1 84813 009 8 Pb

Contents

Acknowledgements

It was Leslie Knott who made this book happen. When she was a student at Reading University, she went down to London looking for books that might be able to explain to her what it was that made Communication for Development so important to so many people. She arrived at Zed Books looking for help. She didn't find the book. What she did find was an interested editor who asked her to suggest people who might be able to write the book she hoped to read – a book that might explain to her the potential of Communication for Development, an applied field of international development.

For Leslie, the search had really begun in Afghanistan. In 2004, she arrived alone in Maimana in the north of the country with the unbelievable task of having to set up a 'women-managed' radio station for the local population. She did not speak Dari. She was in a culture that did not condone women working in a radio station, let alone managing one. She was 28. She had a diploma in journalism from a community college in British Columbia and about three months' experience through a short contract with the Canadian Broadcasting Corporation (CBC). She was employed by a now defunct Vancouver-based organization to set up and operate 'women-managed' radio stations in the post-conflict country. She knew that she needed to learn more about communication.

Wendy and her husband Paul were halfway through a two-year assignment in Kabul. Paul had met Leslie when he went to Maimana, about a year after she arrived. The next time Leslie visited Kabul she went to their house for dinner. At dinner in the garden under the grapevines, another communication colleague pointed Leslie in the direction of the University of Reading for her communication studies – and so the story continues. Leslie suggested to Zed that we be contracted to write the book – and here we are writing away.

Friends, family and colleagues had the patience to edit and critique our drafts; we are very thankful to Noel Salmond, Barbara Bryce, Brendan Quarry, Ursula Nathan, Elin Gynn and Jim Shute, who gave us valuable feedback on the full manuscript. We are also thankful for feedback from Sarah Cardey, Florencia Enghel, Nancy Button, Leslie Knott, Gillian Salmond, Ian Smillie and the Zed editors.

Our network of practitioners and colleagues provided encouragement, case studies, ideas, field support, inspiration and critique. We are thankful to Elena Altieri, Silvia Balit, Brian Beaton, Guy Bessette, Beverly Castillo Herrera, Ashoke Chatterjee, Nimmi Chauhan, Kavita Das Gupta, Eduardo del Río (Rius), Minou Fuglesang, Santiago Funes, Roberta Hilbruner, Kiran Karnak, Paul MacLeod, Gerardo Martínez, Blythe McKay, Gemma Millan, Chris Morry, Joaquin Navas, Olle Nordberg, Kajsa Övergaard, Alex and Wilna Quarmyne, April Pojman, Gaston Roberge, Emrys Shoemaker, Mark Stiles (author of the letter to the professor in Chapter 1), Himalini Verma and Santayan Sengupta of Thoughtshop, and Mark Waldron. You have all helped us inject some 'good' communication into the profession.

Good communication is like a good conversation – it is respectful, mutually beneficial, gives both parties a chance to negotiate and clarify points and leaves people feeling as though the conversation was worthwhile. Sending and receiving is not a good metaphor for communication – communication is not a linear process. It is the dynamics of interaction and negotiated understanding that need to be addressed by communication professionals. (Communication Initiative, 2003)

Introduction

We are practitioners. Between us we have more than forty years' experience either applying communication in bits and pieces throughout various projects or designing full communication initiatives. We are part of a professional and academic community that works and believes in Communication for Development. Yet we have come to realize that we have been acting like a sect – almost like masons in a secret society; we recognize each other by our words. If we can talk so easily to each other, why can't we explain to our friends and relatives what it is that we do? We have seen it work: how is it that we fail to explain its potential?

We recognize the irony: we have been advocates for this field through the type of publications that only converted communicators would read. Our writing has been inaccessible, only academics can endure it, and yet the message was meant for a wider audience. This book is an attempt to break from that habit.

We share what we have to say through stories. Our stories are about *what we know best* – the mistakes, fleeting triumphs and many frustrations that have dogged us throughout our practice. Like many of you, we have the experience of reading glowing reports about projects that did not reflect the reality as we knew it. Who did they think they were kidding? So we decided to restrict our stories to those that we have experienced ourselves, with a few exceptions. In some cases this has led to travel to the field to assure ourselves that our memories have not faltered.

It is amazing to discover how very hard it is to write about communication. Not about the nuts and bolts of the practice – the planning, the audience research, the media and methods. But to get at the essence of communication, the underlying point that makes communication the centre point of whatever it is that constitutes good development – that is the hard part.

When you boil it right down, planning a communication strategy is not rocket science. Nor viewed coldly is it necessarily exciting. This made us question just what it was that had made so many of us dedicate many years to the thankless task of trying to explain the importance of communication to the international development community. Our friend and communication colleague Ashoke Chatterjee puts it bluntly: It is as foolish to have a project without communication as it is to have one without money.

About this book

We have come to believe that it is not communication that makes good development but good development that contains good communication.

This book sets out to unravel this notion. It is divided into three parts. In Part I we describe what we have come to know. We acknowledge the movement away from the development world's fascination with large, obsessively planned results-based approaches. We revisit the core principles from *What Now? Another Development,* a 1975 proposal by the Dag Hammarskjöld Foundation. We dedicate Chapter 2 to exploring how *Another Development* still provides a context for good communication: we call it 'Communication for Another Development'. In Chapter 3 we explore the differences between *planners* and *searchers*: development should be more about exploring and enabling, less about prescribing. In Chapter 4 we try to find out why we communicators have such a hard time explaining what we do.

In Part II we describe the framework we have used to reflect on our experience. This framework has three coordinates: champions, an understanding of context, and communication functions. We relate the trials of what we call 'working in the grey zone'. The 'grey zone' is the sandbox where the conventional development industry allows us to play. So often we find that effective development happens outside this zone – despite the development industry rather than thanks to it. For us the 'grey zone' summarizes all those contracts we agreed to take on where the conditions were not conducive to good communication. We recognize that we have in fact unwittingly forced our communication expertise into short missions only to find our expectations disappear soon after we go. We have been blind to the conditions. We have expected more than could possibly be achieved.

We go on to describe the various ways we have found to navigate the grey zone. We tell stories of the pioneering champions who managed to work their magic. We celebrate today's champions who have taken the principles from the pioneers and adapted them to the current media and challenges. In Chapter 8 we look at the different dimensions of context. We note the value of champions who stay in context. We explain how context so often dictates what is possible.

In Part III we look forward to what we can do differently as practitioners. We dedicate a chapter to several touchstones that guide our decisions. As fast as we write we cannot keep up with the changes and challenges for communication in the information age. While the new technologies are creating an uncharted context, we return to some hardy principles of *Another Development*, of community development and of adult education to provide direction. We do not make predictions, but we are confident that our compass provides *principles that travel* to harness the new technologies.

We have come to understand that the only sustainable aspect of Communication for Development as a field is its constant negotiation for survival. If you look around, the units under this label have largely disappeared from most multilateral organizations. And yet, ironically, the predicament of our planet has never needed communication more. As signs begin to show that globalization is unravelling, new forms of collaboration and networking are giving us hope. In this book we use 'Communication for Another Development' not as a label, but as a marker of a history that is worth revisiting. We are confident that the core principles behind Communication for Development will travel, though its original name may not – by the time you finish this book, you will have worked out your own variation.

ONE

Communication for Development: setting the scene

For centuries, several groups of Inuit have roamed the Canadian Arctic. They depended on the native caribou (wild reindeer) as a source of food, using their hides for clothing and shelter. The hunt was not only a means of survival; success as a hunter was an indication of recognition as a man.

Since the 1950s, biologists from southern Canada have spent millions of dollars observing the habits of the caribou. They monitored the state of the different herds in the Keewatin area of the far north, part of what is now known as Nunavut. They usually didn't bother to report their findings to the people of the north. When they did, it was in a scientific language quite foreign to the Inuit.

In the 1970s, mining exploration began extensively in the Keewatin district, bringing with it people, equipment, aircraft and noise. The Inuit became alarmed. They believed that the noise was hurting the caribou, driving them from their traditional feeding areas. The miners and biologists thought otherwise. Public hearings took place with Inuit filing lawsuits to stop the mining. While these failed to halt the mining operations, more rigid conditions were put on mining activities to protect the caribou. At the same time, the biologists gave information suggesting the government also impose strict quotas on the hunting of the Kaminuriak herd. An angry impasse occurred.

The crisis came to a head when an Inuit leader reacted to new game laws and declared a state of war between his people and the biologists and game wardens. There was a call for the Inuit to defy new game quotas. Hostilities heightened on both sides.

Alarmed at the gravity of the situation, a government official called in Donald Snowden – the man who had pioneered the use of video as a communication method to facilitate community dialogue. Snowden proposed a solution. He suggested that each group be videotaped in their own domain in the appropriate language. This would allow each to give full rein to feelings and explanations in the language of choice. He stipulated that every tape produced be available to all groups and that editing rights be vested only with those who appear on tape – not in Inuit organizations, nor with senior government officials.

Two production crews were assembled – Inuit and non-Inuit – and training was given to augment the crew experience. A system was put in place to select community representatives from each of the Inuit communities to act as spokespeople for the communities. Four biologists were selected to speak on behalf of the scientific community. Following production, all videotapes were versioned into the second language for playback. The tapes were then collected and played back to separate discussion groups of Inuit and government people. Each group could experience the tapes in their own language.

So rich was the material on the tapes that they were taken back to the communities for screening and discussion. People met in homes, schools, community halls and at social gatherings to watch, to learn and to comment. Over time major changes of attitude were seen to take place and people expressed a willingness to work together with government in resolution of problems around the Kaminuriak herd. Similarly biologists screened tapes. So impressed were they by the tone and content of Inuit knowledge that there was an agreement that a new understanding had been reached where both groups could work together.

Initially, the government extended an invitation to the Inuit leaders to sit on the already formed government committee. This invitation was rejected. Instead, Inuit leaders formed their own committee and invited government to sit with them. There was a realization that this was an important turning point in the debate and soon government agreed to abolish the old system and join the newly formed Inuit committee. Today, more than twenty years after that first initiative, the Beverly and Qamanirjuaq (Kaminuriak) Caribou Management Board is still operational; its website (www.arctic-caribou.com) opening note is a testament to the enduring impact of that first intervention: 'Welcome to the Beverly and Quamanirjuaq Caribou Management Board, a group of hunters, biologists and wildlife managers working together to conserve Canada's vast Beverly and Qamanirjuaq caribou herds for the welfare of traditional caribou-using communities and others.'

We use this example, from almost forty years ago, to illustrate the power of Communication for Development. The story is compelling: you can see the Inuit and the biologists watching each other's videos. You can imagine how they began to change their understanding. You can appreciate how the medium (video) made it possible for each side to listen to the other's story in their own language without interruption – for once. The Kaminuriak Caribou Herd case shows how a cultural, social and economic disagreement between traditional users of resources and scientists was overcome. This is communication at its best.

A field known by many names

While we like to use such examples to introduce the term 'Communication for Development', we stress that this is only one approach among many variations and numerous definitions that go by that name. Like a chameleon, communication is embedded in international development. It changes colour to reflect the development thinking of the day: Development Support Communication, Development Communication, Communication for Human Development, Social Communication, Communication for Social Change, Strategic Communication – the list goes on.

These labels also work as markers of international development eras, each trying to capture its relevance and reflecting the dominant thinking of the day (Nederveen Pieterse, 2001). The term 'Communication for Development' was prominently used as the title of the first World Congress on Communication for Development (WCCD) in 2006 organized by the Communication Initiative, FAO and the World

Bank. Now even this is being supplanted by the formulistic-sounding C4D (UNICEF) or DevCom (World Bank). The different names have caused exasperation and confusion among practitioners and students in this field. So, too, do the variety of communication approaches and methodologies that have emerged. One communication colleague mocked the confusion by drafting this fake letter:

Dear Professor

As a student of yours over the past year, I must confess that I am confused: I don't understand what the subject of your course is really all about. You are now talking about social communication. Last week, it was communication for social change – I thought I knew what that was. By the way, which is correct: is it communication or communications, with an 's'? I'm really perplexed by that one.

I read the background literature you gave me and it refers to development communication, well not always, sometimes it's 'communication for development' or when I read that UNDP paper, it's 'development support communication'. I thought I understood what that was all about until I read Neill McKee's book. He said that communication for development (or was that development communication?) sometimes involves TRAINING. *TRAINING*, what's that got to do with communication?!!

Speaking of training, I understand that you are conducting a workshop on 'participatory communication' in June here in Ottawa. Is that the same as '*social* communication' or is it more like 'communication for social change'?

I read the book by Kotler that you recommended. It was all about 'social marketing.' I learned that some communication practitioners *sell* social products and behaviours in the same way that Madison Avenue ad firms *market* fashion and cosmetics. Hey, that's a neat idea.

But then I went to the Johns Hopkins website and I really got confused. They were talking about using 'info-tainment' and 'enter-education' to control population growth. (Boy, I can't wait until I 'exit-education' – this is too confusing and a bit scary.)

I went to the World Bank for enlightenment and found many references to 'BCC' – Behavioural Change Communication. That has a World Bank ring to it, doesn't it? It reminded me a little of what I saw on CNN recently – how the US military used communication to convince Iraqi troops to surrender. But they called that 'PsyOps', Psychological Operations.

By the way, Professor, what is the difference between BCC and IEC? And while you're at, how do BCC and IEC relate to ICTs?
Your perplexed and bewildered student,

[Name withheld]

A bit of history

In the early 1970s, while Don Snowden was in Canada using video to foster dialogue and facilitate conflict-resolution, Nora Quebral, professor emeritus from the University of the Philippines and pioneer in this field, was applying communication techniques to disseminating agricultural information to poor farmers in the Philippines. Erskine Childers picked up the idea. Childers, an Irish communication specialist, brought the idea of development communication to the United Nations Development Programme (UNDP) and to UNICEF, through his successful work in combating bilharzia in Egypt. In the late 1960s Childers and Thai sociologist Mallica Vajrathon established the first UN-funded Development Communication Support Service for Asia in Bangkok (Fraser and Restrepo-Estrada, 1998).

Soon after, the UN Food and Agriculture Organization (FAO) set up a Development Support Communication Branch at its headquarters in Rome. Since then, other UN organizations (UNICEF, UNFPA, WHO) have established development communication units supporting the dissemination and adoption of health practices. Often known as Information, Education and Communication (IEC), these initiatives have mobilized communities around childhood immunization, family planning and nutrition. UNESCO in particular emphasized the importance of the mass media and sought to enhance public service broadcasting.

At present, UN organizations and other donor agencies are pouring money into communication initiatives to combat the spread of HIV/AIDS and eliminate polio. Development agencies, like the UK Department for International Development (DFID), are allocating funds for communication across all research projects. Each agency interprets communication to suit its particular interests. Come to think of it, we have two reasons to explain why the field goes by many names: academics and practitioners contest its theoretical foundations, and development agencies use it for different purposes. No wonder it is hard to explain.

In their book *Communicating for Development* (1998), Colin Fraser, the first head of FAO's communication for development unit, and Sonia Restrepo-Estrada, a Colombian communication specialist, provide what in our view is one of the more comprehensive definitions to date:

> Communication for development is the use of communication processes, techniques and media to help people toward a full awareness of their situation and their options for change, to resolve conflicts, to work towards consensus, to help people plan actions for change and sustainable development, to help people acquire the knowledge and skills they need to improve their condition and that of society, and to improve the effectiveness of institutions. (Fraser and Restrepo-Estrada, 1998: 63)

What do we like about it? The definition begins by emphasizing process over product. It places techniques and media at the service of development where what counts is enhancing people's ability to manage their own lives. It acknowledges the different objectives that drive communication. It places communication for development squarely in support of another approach to development.

Entering the field: which door to choose?

We entered this field through work and applied projects in the field. Wendy got her start with the Canadian Broadcasting Corporation in Canada and continued with an internship with Radio Sutatenza in Colombia in 1981. Ricardo began by making drawings with farmers about new agricultural practices – as it happens also in Colombia in 1983 – and went from there to work in the FAO unit in Rome. Each practitioner we know has a similar story: each has entered through a different door.

If you are a development planner, you will be interested in media management, how to connect with different audiences using different media combinations, how to develop a communication campaign. You will wonder what percentage of a project budget needs to be allocated

to communication and how to evaluate its effectiveness. You will probably take a short course offered by a consultancy firm in this field.

If you are a field practitioner, you will be attracted to a specific
medium and set of skills: video or digital photography, popular theatre,
scriptwriting for radio or graphic art for printed materials. You might
be attracted to participatory approaches where the audience is involved
in both choosing the content and preparing the materials. You will be
keen to try out different communication aids in support of training
or using media to listen to what people already know. If you have a
background in participation you will be pleased to discover an overlap
with some communication approaches. The emphasis on learning
what people already know is common to both. In communication we
go a step further to investigate existing ways in which people already
exchange information, and we are on the lookout for methods and
media that can be improved or introduced.

If you are a journalist you may be wondering how to adapt your
knowledge of radio and television into the development field. You
might well think that producing a programme on a development
theme is what it will take. Then you sit down and think through
what it is you are actually trying to do and realize that providing
information is but one step, among many, in a long process.

If you are a student at university, you will be introduced to the
theoretical underpinnings and the foundational authors and books,
such as Daniel Lerner's *The Passing of Traditional Society: Modernizing the Middle East* (1958); Everett Rogers's *Diffusion of Innovations*
(1962); and Wilbur Schramm's *Mass Media and National Development*
(1964) (see McAnany, 2008). No doubt you will discover the debate
between diffusion and participation. You will be introduced to the
many writings around the issue, culminating in the giant tome
produced by the Communication for Social Change Consortium: an
anthology with a collection of historical and contemporary teadings
to take you on a journey from Bertolt Brecht to the present day
(Gumucio-Dagron and Tufte, 2006).

No matter what door you use to enter, you will soon find that your
role as a communication professional is that of understudy to the
main star – water and sanitation, irrigation, natural resource management, health and so on. Often we are called in to 'fix' a problem
when the first approach has not worked well. In development banks,

communication is relegated to the back seat (Mefalopulos, 2008). Silvio Waisbord describes communication as always playing 'second fiddle' in international development (Waisbord, 2007). He dubs it a 'guest discipline' that functions in organizations pursuing other goals (health, agriculture etc.) and as such is seen as only offering tactical support. It commands, he says, as much respect as cocktail piano music among jazz cognoscenti.

So much communication and so little understanding

The irony in this field is that the word 'communication' has many interpretations. This leads to the confusion so evident in the letter to the professor. The different interpretations stem from a variety of myths: (1) communication can be improvised any time; (2) communication is the same as medium; (3) communication units in agencies have a clear mandate; (4) communication is about sending information; and (5) information will do the job. We have separated these for clarity although in reality they tend to merge. You will notice how each feeds on the other.

MYTH 1: COMMUNICATION CAN BE IMPROVISED ANY TIME

The idea of actually having to plan for a communication input, researching different audience perspectives and 'packaging' the message (or product) began to take hold in the mid-1960s. The world was by then used to the power of advertising, but the idea of using advertising techniques to market social change was a new concept. One of the many ideas borrowed from the commercial world was the need to research the intended audiences.

> In the commercial world, the marketer must know the audience in order to gain some small advantage over the competition. He or she does not aim at an amorphous mass but learns a great deal about the audience – facts such as gender, ages, income levels, social class and lifestyles – in order to price and promote the product in a way that is consistent with these characteristics. (McKee, 1992: 10)

McKee's example shows how the international development world adopted marketing methods for social development. Social marketing became popular among agencies and projects where behaviour change was the main purpose of their communication (Kotler and Roberto, 1989). This implied that the agency had something to 'sell' and the audience needed to listen and learn about the benefits of the idea. In some cases – the global polio eradication campaign, for example – it can work well when people understand the message, are willing to change behaviour (allow their child to be inoculated) and have easy access to a vaccination clinic. Even this does not always work, as we shall see later in the book. There are other cases – HIV/AIDS, for example – when this approach is much less effective, as described further in Chapter 7.

The basic steps needed for planning a communication effort are important for any kind of communication, including the participatory kind. We include examples in this book that illustrate the importance of audience research. We emphasize the need to work within what the Brazilian adult education and communication specialist Paulo Freire called the reality of people's existing knowledge; to use their preferred media, to use the language and images that make sense to them.

MYTH 2: COMMUNICATION IS THE SAME AS MEDIUM

When Ricardo worked at FAO, rarely a week went by without someone from a technical unit requesting a video or a radio programme. When he asked who it was for, what those audiences already knew and what media they had access to (the basic questions in communications planning), he was told that assessing all of that would be too costly; they just wanted the video. The video – a media product – was enough for them. However, we have learned that the process is just as important; without it the media product will easily miss its mark.

Wendy cites a different case in Pakistan. Here the manager of a water project decided that it might be 'useful' to provide a documentary video on water use. Without any research or thought as to what the video would achieve, a producer was hired and the video was put together at great expense. After one showing to less-than-interested water-sector decision-makers, the video remained on a shelf – testimony to a misunderstanding of what the communication intervention would actually achieve. Had the manager been honest about his desire for a video, he would have said that he wanted a video to show the funding agency that he was doing his job and had something to show for it. In other words, it was public relations camouflaged as a product to show decision-makers (and anyone else) the importance of community-managed water projects. An output rather than an outcome, to use current development-speak.

What was the point except that it was fun to make and the manager had a 'product' to show for the money? It is amazing how often this still happens and how much money is wasted producing such media products that are rarely used.

MYTH 3: COMMUNICATION UNITS IN AGENCIES HAVE A CLEAR MANDATE

This lack of clarity in Myth 2 is exacerbated when the communications units in development agencies do not have a clear mandate. People and organizations say they are doing one thing but are actually presenting something quite different. Some agencies have 'communication units' to handle the communication needs of the institution. These units are often asked to handle both the organizational public relations needs *and* participatory communication for development: a somewhat schizophrenic approach to two fields that are simply not the same. They require different skills and talent, and are often the antithesis of one another.

Today, there seems to be increasing confusion between public relations, information, knowledge management, social marketing and the participatory forms of communication.

MYTH 4: COMMUNICATION IS SIMPLY SENDING MESSAGES

Our planet is immersed in mass media that constantly bombard us with messages. We are the target of commercial, military and cultural propaganda through every medium available. As Marshall McLuhan wrote, we are so immersed that our very thought process and language are shaped by the media (McLuhan, 1965). As a result many people have started to assume that those messages are communication, when they are not. The mindset prevails that communication is public relations; that it is about reaching out to tell people about who *you* are and what *you do*, and why *you matter so much*. This situation exists just as much in the international development industry.

The development industry sees communication as the transfer of information from one group of people to another, the assumption being that if they know what we know change will follow. Cees Hamelink, an academic in the Netherlands, notes that this belief reflects the dominant development paradigm – an interventionist approach with resources and information as input, and social development as output. Yet communication and information are not the same. This is not theoretical hair-splitting: it is a substantial distinction between sending information in different formats, and people exchanging ideas and values through dialogue (Waisbord, 2007).

MYTH 5: INFORMATION WILL DO THE JOB

We are reminded that 'most assumptions about the role and effects of information and knowledge are based upon a seriously flawed cause–effect model' (Hamelink, 2002: 7). The idea that lack of information is the main reason that people do not adopt a particular behaviour has long been disproved:

> Research on adolescent pregnancy illustrates another dimension of the knowledge use problem. In a classic study, adolescent health specialist Michael Resnik ... interviewed teenagers who became pregnant. He found very few cases in which the problem was a lack of information about contraception, about pregnancy, or about how to avoid pregnancies. The problem was the teens just didn't apply what they knew. 'There is an incredible gap between the knowledge and the application of that knowledge. In so many instances it's heartbreaking – they have the knowledge, the awareness, and the understanding, but somehow it does not apply to them.' (Patton, 2008: 8, quoting Resnick 1984: 5)

Nowhere has this become more apparent than in the struggle to understand how to combat HIV/AIDS. The sense of urgency surrounding this battle has placed communication centre stage and pushed communicators to think further and deeper into the importance of culture, gender, age, power structure and community as influencers more potent than a piece of information. We have to learn to focus on the forest and not just on the trees (Singhal, 2003).

Context matters: no one-size-fits-all

Think about how often donors and governments like to talk about 'best practices'. This thinking reflects an industrial, engineering way of looking at the world; it is part of the reason why we refer to the international development 'industry' in this book. Our challenge is that these recipes do not work. Context matters and solutions need to be designed to fit the local situation. Without an understanding of context communication initiatives will fall short of their objectives. We invite you to contrast the following examples.

In 1971, Prince Philip, the Duke of Edinburgh, caused an uproar in Canada. He attacked Canadians in their House of Commons, calling them physically unfit and not in any position to respond to an emergency. The government was moved to action. It worked with Corporate Canada to form a small and independent non-profit organization. By happenstance a staff member put together the words 'participation' and 'action' and the name 'Participaction' was born (it worked well bilingually). The aim was to use the media to get individual Canadians physically fit (and, by corollary, build a fit nation).

How did they do it? Participaction relied on modern marketing techniques to get their message across. They carried out market research through carefully constructed focus groups across the country. They quickly 'branded' the name Participaction and created easy and fun ways to get Canadians active. They focused on the fifteen-minute workout and devised clever ways to get Canadians to 'walk a block'. Their first ad compared a 30-year-old Canadian's level of fitness to that of a 60-year-old Swede. This ad played for fifteen seconds during the football season on television. Canadians were alarmed and embarrassed. This was followed by self-deprecating bus signs 'The True North Soft and Free'. Participaction supplemented media campaigns by joining with schools and the sport clubs. They used intermediaries to get schools to compete with each other on fitness days. Later Participaction set up a Participaction Challenge pitting one city against another; Participaction staff were shown making mock arrests of mayors who were deemed unfit. Pressure was put on politicians, educators and the public – and it worked.

Participaction worked through many factors. The social context was extremely important. Canadians tend to self-effacement and mockery of their self-image – it wasn't difficult to create slogans that played to this national characteristic. At the same time, the culture is inculcated with the sense that each person is almost directly responsible for his/her own health. This made it easy to convey a sense of duty to 'get out and participate'. Finally the opportunity to take fifteen minutes to exercise was made accessible and easy – the government, the school boards and the workplace collaborated to make it possible.

Contrast this to a hygiene education programme that was part of a World Bank water and sanitation programme in Chittagong, Bang-ladesh. In the late 1980s Wendy accompanied a World Bank mission to this eastern city in Bangladesh. Her job was to assess the impact of the hygiene education programme in a water and sanitation project in one of the crowded bustis (slums) of the city. It was the middle of the rainy season. Every day she walked the narrow pathways of the slum community and spoke with householders. Twice daily she watched the water from the nearby river rise to cover the floor of each hut. She watched the women rush to put their belongings in the rafters to avoid the water and watched the children continue playing in the mud. She recorded the broken handpumps and the abandoned latrines. She learned about the absentee landlords and the struggle to maintain the rent. The idea of having an aid worker coming to teach hygiene education in this context, she thought, verged on the absurd.

But what if the team or a leader in the community had sat with individuals, or groups of householders, and discussed with them their concerns or ideas for improving the situation. Would hygiene education be on their immediate agenda? Probably not, but what might emerge would be an expression of what the householders see as a first practical step towards an improvement in their daily lives.

We use the Participaction and the Chittagong examples to il-lustrate how each context demands its own tailor-made approach. In both cases, however, some common principles apply: begin working with what people already know; understand how they perceive their predicament; do not impose solutions; work with the method and media they prefer; be prepared to make mistakes; engage people as much as is practical.

This brings us back to the essence of the Kaminuriak Herd example, which explains the notion of participatory communication, lately also referred to as 'Communication for Social Change'. People usually know what is best for them. The role of the communicator here is to believe that and be open to the possibility for dialogue, listening and discussion. As Snowden remarked, the mere act of using the video and focusing on the issue helped soften the antagonists and paved the way for listening and discussion (Quarry, 1994).

Enough messages, more listening

Inasmuch as 'communication' has been equated with public relations and marketing, its listening and advocacy dimensions have been pushed aside. Hamelink writes of development as being something 'other' than the delivery of resources. Contrary to the conventional approach, he suggests that foremost on the development agenda should be the capacity to facilitate social dialogue.

> It should be the foremost priority on the development agenda to develop the capacity for social dialogue. To solve the world's most pressing problems, people do not need more volumes of information and knowledge – they need to acquire the capacity to talk to each other across boundaries of culture, religion and language... This sounds obvious and facile. In reality however the dialogue is an extremely difficult form of speech. In many societies people have neither time nor patience for dialogical communication. The dialogue requires the capacity to listen, to be silent, to suspend judgment, to critically investigate one's own assumptions, to ask reflexive question and to be open to change. The dialogue has no short-term and certain outcome. This conflicts with the spirit of modern achievement-oriented societies. (Hamelink, 2002: 8)

Father Gaston Roberge, a Canadian communication practitioner and teacher in Kolkata, sums up this dilemma by describing how the words 'communication', 'development' and 'development communication' have been used to mean several things – at times at odds among themselves:

> For some, development is simply a matter of imitating the achievements of the so-called developed countries; whereas for others, development is the unfolding of harmony among people living in justice, in conversation and in respect of their physical environment...

For some, communication is mainly a transfer of messages, while for others it is mainly a matter of achieving communication through conversation...

For some, development communication is mainly a transfer of information or knowledge leading to desired changes in behaviour; in that view communication is merely instrumental, whereas for others, development communication is itself part of the development process. (Roberge, 2003: 2)

Unpacking the debate

We have found it useful to sketch out a typology of communication approaches to help explain the variety of ways that communication is embedded in development. For example we acknowledge the importance of public relations, but we see it distinct from the need to raise awareness or provide information. Promoting an organization is different from helping people understand the value of immunization or information surrounding a new water policy. This can be done using social marketing for behavioural change. However, this is very different from the participatory examples, such as the Kaminuriak case, where communication helped people understand others' perspectives; there was no pre-packaged solution to sell, just a process of dialogue. The following basic list of communication functions covers the range of purposes: public relations, awareness-raising, behaviour change, advocacy and participation. Further differentiations and their theoretical background are explained in the literature (Mefalopulos, 2008; Morris, 2003; Waisbord, 2001).

What matters most is to have clarity around the purpose of the communication initiative – the overall 'intent'. What is it that the communication initiative is trying to do and what do we hope it will achieve?

We mentioned that Communication for Development has been a battlefield between the diffusion and modernization perspective of development and the participation and dependency one (Morris, 2003). The first theory was developed by Everett Rogers with the launching of his book *The Diffusion of Innovations* in 1962. In it he emphasized his belief that societies that adopted modern technologies would overcome their development barriers. While his ideas evolved over time (and Rogers released several editions), the book set the tone for a way of thinking that suggested the developed North had the know-how to fix the underdeveloped South.

In many parts of the world the reaction to the diffusion approach challenged the notion of modernization. Academics and practitioners from both the North and the South argued that the problem instead was one of political, economic and military dependency. What the South demanded was self-determination and more participation in managing its own development (Melkote, 2002). Many of these ideas were encapsulated in the mid-1970s in a proposal entitled *What Now? Another Development*, an alternative approach put forward by the Dag Hammarskjöld Foundation. We explore this proposal in the next chapter.

The critics shifted attention away from technology to a political debate about power and dependency (Díaz Bordenave, 1977). An important part of the foundational thinking came from adult education. Paulo Freire differentiated between 'extension', as the one-way transmission of information, and 'communication', as the two-way exchange of perspectives leading to what he called 'conscientization' (Freire, 1973). Participatory communication joined forces with participatory research and action research, and in turn also contributed methods (Anyaegbunam et al., 2004; Bessette, 2004). People's abilities and knowledge were seen to be the basis for change, hence the need to have them participate in defining what development should mean to their lives. The response emerged in different part of the world, and with multiple variations (Bessette, 2004; Chambers, 1997, 2005; White, 1999; White et al., 1994). We cannot do justice to the wealth of ideas and innovations that led to the notion of participatory communication. We know of one case where this was done, and it took over 1,000 pages to tell the story (Gumucio-Dagron and Tufte, 2006).

Jan Servaes and Patchanee Malikhao, communication thinkers from the Netherlands and Thailand, lament that, despite an evolution of thinking, most communication initiatives still focus on the diffusion model. Most still focus on message delivery, informing the population about projects, illustrating the advantage of these projects, and recommending that they be supported. The point of departure for the participatory model, they point out, must be the community. It is at the community level that the problems of living conditions are discussed, and interactions with other communities are elicited. This principle implies the right to participation in the planning and production of media content (Servaes and Malikhao, 2004).

In this book we come to understand the different conceptualizations of development through our communication lens. Through our experiences we illustrate how communication is stranded in this polarization and how some communication functions live happily in one camp but not in the other. We see more potential for our applied field in another, alternative, and more participatory development. Jan Nederveen Pieterse, an academic from the Netherlands, points out that alternative development lacks a theoretical framework (Nederveen Pieterse, 2001). We do not attempt to meet this challenge. Our contribution towards participatory development comes from our experience and reflections in Communication for Development.

Turning decades of advocacy work on its head

The Participaction example illustrates the power of communication for behavioural change. We use this example because we find that it explains what the international development domain has come to expect in terms of communication for development. It illustrates how a well-designed campaign, which utilizes media intelligently, and which orchestrates other tangible action on the ground, can lead to awareness-raising and behavioural change. The Kaminuriak example, on the other hand, is different. It shows how communication can function as a method to help people express their own needs, break social barriers and redress power imbalances.

In a way, it is ironic that today the communication field is increasingly popular. Corporations continue to spend significant funds in this direction, and so do governments, think-tanks and the military. But the importance of staking territory, expanding influence and maintaining political profile has eclipsed the 'listening' side of communication. The function of communication that nurtures our self-awareness and sense of confidence, the one that helps us understand and change our situation in our own terms, has lost ground and credibility.

This book is dedicated to putting the 'listening' function back on centre stage, to celebrating existing examples of such an understanding of communication, and to understanding the conditions and factors that led to their success.

If you think of development as something more than an increase in income, or GDP – and most people do – it becomes clear that the centre of any development initiative has to be the people who are involved in its benefits. Developing a plan is one thing but getting people to implement a plan is something completely separate. Again most would agree. But when you ask 'whose plan is it anyway?' and 'what do the people who are the subject of the plan actually want for themselves?' you run into messiness. Most planners cannot cope with messiness. It takes time, money and a whole lot of adaptability (noticeably in short supply among governments and donors). It takes a disposition to listen.

The communication definition we used from Fraser and Restrepo-Estrada (1998), however, suggests something different. It proposes that communication media (radio, video) and tools (dialogue between people) can serve a different purpose. They can be used to help people facilitate their own discussion of their own predicament leading to their own plan of action. This implies a much more people-centred and bottom-up approach that will not necessarily fit into an overall plan prepared by others. This, in fact, suggests *another* approach to development.

Take the following example from Tanzania. As part of an evaluation contract, we interviewed the director of a health project with an impressive background in his field, years of experience and no communication training. Yet his project used communication methods and media in an effective manner. He was candid about the project, he was most respectful of his national colleagues, and he had been in the country close to a decade. We note that quite often effective communication emerges when the conditions are right. Our emphasis on the conditions and the key people (the champions) is a break from our past emphasis on the methods and media. Exceptions exist. Communication *can* be the source of innovation; it certainly often does create the conditions for change. Nevertheless, we wish to present the view that good communication will only emerge through a compelling case for better development.

This book turns decades of communication advocacy on its head. Many academics and practitioners – we included – have been writing scholarly papers with pleas for more communication components to be built into development programmes. Now we have come to see it differently and want to illustrate this new vantage point. We realize it is not communication that creates effective (good) development. Instead, a different approach to development is the condition for good communication.

PART I

What we know

TWO

The meaning of
'another' development

When we talk about good communication we are really expressing an attitude to development. In this way the word 'communication' becomes a proxy for addressing the need for another development. It has taken us quite a while to be aware of this.

For many years we thought that any international development project would be greatly improved by building in a planned communication strategy. This is true up to a point. Lately, we have come to understand that we should be looking at it the other way around – it is in fact good development that breeds good communication. And right now good development seems to have been left behind.

An article by Jonathan Harr in the *New Yorker*, 'Lives of the Saints', describes the trials of humanitarian workers living near Darfur on the Chad side of the border. He quotes from a 2005 institutional analysis of the United Nations High Commission for Refugees (UNHCR) describing the organizational culture as having 'a tendency to behave as though its primary purpose is, for example, to create reports, arrange staff movements and keep itself funded', rather than 'protecting and assisting refugees' (Harr, 2009: 55). Substitute UNHCR for just about any other UN agency or bilateral donor – the same applies. Come to think of it, bureaucracy has increased exponentially with the use of the computer and Internet. This has

been happening since the late 1980s. All of us have our favourite
stories; this one is from Wendy.

Paul's briefcase

My husband Paul does not have a bureaucratic bone in his body.
A product of the 1960s, he moved from Notting Hill in London
(selling antiques) to Egypt (drawing on sidewalks) to Morocco (who
knows) to Canada, where I tried to get him to think first (and learn
to plan). In the mid-eighties, when we were living in Ghana, the
Canadian International Development Agency (CIDA) hired him to
set up and manage the first Administrative Support Unit for their
personnel living in Ghana. The work covered just about everything
you can think of to tend to the administrative needs for all the
Canadian-funded projects in the country. This ranged from handling sea shipments at the harbour in Tema, to fixing the plumbing
in houses, to going to the airport to meet consultants. Just about
every evening he would wind up perched on a seat at the bar set up
in the Canadian club, his battered briefcase lying on the floor at his
feet. Since everyone knew they would find him there, consultants
would arrive and ask him for their passports or visas. Paul would dig
into the briefcase and hand them out. They grew to expect this.
    A few years after we left Ghana, I bumped into a consultant
who knew Paul in Ghana. He told me that everyone missed him.
He said that the person who replaced him was in essence a systems
man – a person really into the computer. Consequently, the whole
Administrative Support Unit was computerized and systems were
put in place to track passports, shipments and so on (a good thing).
But, the consultant went on, whenever anyone would ask the new
director where they could find their passports, he would point to the
screen and search the location – in another office, still in the police
station, wherever, but never there on the table ready for taking.
    Fast-forward twenty years. I am sitting in a coffee shop in
London having lunch with a friend recently retired from the
British Department for International Development. He is telling
me the story of his arrival in Nigeria, where, he said, he walked
into the DFID office to find everyone sitting staring at their
computer screens, and by corollary not going out to see the country

– they were, he said, disappearing up their own arses on matrix management.

He told how he immediately turned right around and walked out. He grabbed a car and driver and drove into the countryside. When they found a few villages, he told the driver to stop. He got out of the car and strode into a village to tell a few surprised villagers that he was 'there to learn'. The elders appeared to be honoured and organized a mass meeting. Much later, back in the office someone took a decision to focus on justice. But, said he, I never found a village interested in that subject – they had their own justice.

Speaking 'another'

Paul has a searching instinct and a common sense to get things done. Wendy's British friend's visit to the village was about making development work on the basis of seeking people out and listening to needs. Both make sense. Yet, keeping things simple and practical in international development has become rare. The common sense is gone. This is where the notion of 'Another Development' has renewed meaning.

Cast your mind back to the mid-1970s. That was when Andreas Fuglesang – a Norwegian communication specialist – collaborated with the Dag Hammarskjöld Foundation of Sweden to produce the report *What Now? Another Development* (1975). The report, prepared to coincide with the Seventh Special Session of the United Nations Assembly, set out new parameters for development thinking. It suggested that the eradication of poverty was not simply about growth. While many of us take that thinking for granted today, it has not necessarily permeated the institutions.

What Now? Another Development was based on five core principles: (1) that development be geared to the satisfaction of needs, beginning with the eradication of poverty; (2) that it be endogenous and self-reliant – that is, relying on the strengths of the societies that undertake it; (3) that it be in harmony with the environment; (4) the need for structural transformations. Structure refers to patterns of ownership over domestic resources that reproduce unequal economic relations at the international level.

Any attempt to change this situation depends on the vision, the will and the organizing capacity of those concerned. It implies that they become self-reliant, that they transform the structures which have brought about the present situation, and that they establish the conditions in which the majority poor will have the means to improve their lot. Such a reform affects both socio-economic and political structures, as well as the linkages between them. (Dag Hammarskjöld Foundation, 1975: 38).

Finally, (5) it stated that immediate action was both necessary and possible.

Fuglesang wrote several books on communication that complemented the Dag Hammarskjöld Foundation work. Sven Hamrell, the executive director of the Foundation acknowledged the Fuglesang contribution to the thinking behind *What Now? Another Development*. In his preface to Fuglesang's most famous book, *About Understanding: Ideas and Observations on Cross-Cultural Communication* (1982), Sven wrote:

It was his unfailing trust in people, his advocacy of people's ability to decide the direction of their development and his demonstration of solutions found by people that helped shape the notion of Another Development.

About Understanding became a seminal book in the field of Communication for Development. With the support of the Foundation, Fuglesang and his wife Dale Chandler went on to organize the 1983 and 1984 workshops on 'Methods and Media for Community Participation'. Those events – and many of the people who contributed to them – set the tone for over two decades of communication practice on which we now reflect. (Most of the drawings in this book were prepared by Ricardo for the workshops.)

This brings us to the core idea of this book: *It is not good communication that makes good development; it is good development that breeds good communication.*

As mentioned in the previous chapter, the World Congress on Communication for Development was held in Rome in 2006. A major focus was helping decision-makers understand and adopt Communication for Development. It was a watershed but in an unexpected way. Through writing for the Congress, Wendy began to see that perhaps decision-makers didn't 'get' participatory communication because that is not what they wanted. They understood it all right but they simply did not want participation to confuse their plans (Quarry, 2006). This led us to further thinking about the context within which a development initiative takes place. Perhaps we have taken hold of the wrong end of the stick.

As practitioners we have often promoted the field on the basis of the methods and media. We hear ourselves saying such thing as 'If you use popular theatre, you will engage the audience as they identify with the characters, and stimulate critical thinking.' We have pushed the methods and media like magic bullets. However, methods and media are but instruments in a wider context. Politics, power, religion, institutions, policies and personalities set the scene. For our methods and media to play a role, we need an enabling context. We need Another (good) Development.

Two years after Andreas Fuglesang published his book, Father Gaston Roberge wrote a book with a similar title: *Another Cinema for Another Society*. Roberge advocated that the kind of cinema that was needed had to be *other* than and *different* from the bulk of the cinema of the time. Another cinema, he wrote, would be committed to the building of another society. He argued that cinema at that time portrayed the life and times of only a select group of society. Another cinema had to be allowed to grow and be inclusive of the reality of the lives of people and societies at the margin.

Gaston and Andreas were both speaking the same language. Both were people committed to creating the conditions for people to decide on their own development. These two champions were not the only ones by any means. We happen to have a collection of them. They excel at using the communication and media technologies of the day. They are critical thinkers, unhappy with the way development has been going off-track – hence the talk about 'another' way of working. The idea seems to be very much alive: in January 2009 we heard of the launch in Guatemala of a book entitled *Otra comunicación para otro desarrollo* (*Another Communication for Another Development*) (Gularte Cosenza et al., 2008).

Communication for Another Development, our title, is the way we convey this rediscovery. *What Now? Another Development* called for helping people improve their lives in their own terms. Intrinsic to this is the role of communication. It is simply not possible to implement this approach to development without enhanced communication between all involved in the process.

The 'Methods and Media for Community Participation' workshops brought together practitioners from around the world to share ideas and methodologies for using communication to effect the principles of *Another Development*. Some were using microscopes to help villagers in Africa learn about parasites. Others demonstrated the power of popular theatre, rural radio and drawing to work with illiterate communities. Tragically, Don Snowden, the Canadian pioneer whom we celebrate in this book, died just months before the second gathering. Snowden had been working with Andreas and the Foundation preparing material for the workshop. It was his suggestion that the second workshop be held in Labrador. In the following quotation he illustrates what 'Communication for Another Development' can achieve. He speaks about the Fogo Process, a case where video and film helped communities come together, which we detail later in the book:

> Today few people on Fogo speak about the filming, yet many believe their lives were changed enormously by it. This can never be accurately measured. But it is certain that the fishermen formed an island-wide producer's cooperative which handled and processed large catches, enabling them to keep the profits on their island. Unemployment of able bodied men disappeared, and government directed their efforts to helping people to stay.... Film did not do these things: people did them. There is little doubt, however, that film created an awareness and self-confidence that was needed for people-advocated development to occur. (Quarry, 1994: 17)

What does Another Development look like?

Finding examples of 'Another Development' turns out to be harder than expected: they need to be about poverty eradication; they should be endogenous and self-reliant; and they must be in harmony with the environment. And on top of that they must contribute to structural transformation and demonstrate immediate action. Ricardo provides a couple of examples.

Eleven years ago I was the co-founder of a small organization where we tried to do development based on local needs and demands. We called it simply the International Support Group. We registered the organization and gradually managed to secure funding to organize workshops to help rural communities gain more control over how they managed their natural resources. In one instance we obtained funding from Danish foreign aid and agreed to organize training workshops on demand from farmers in East Africa. We accepted only 20 per cent of an agreed project budget to travel to the region and make our proposal known. We promised to return the remainder to Danida if we did not get requests from local groups. As we will see later, this was an attempt to work outside what we call the 'grey zone', to be more congruent with the notion of endogenous development.

As it happened, a group of Kenyan organizations took up our challenge and we returned to run a workshop in the Nyeri highlands. The workshop brought together all the main actors in natural resource management into the same room. We spent several days negotiating how farmers, researchers, extension workers and government could collaborate to improve farm production and market access. We dedicated much time to clarify exactly how the different organizations would work together. The methods were not new; many of them were adapted from participatory methodologies. What was different was the fact that the Kenyan stakeholders had organized themselves to make this happen and we had responded (Lightfoot et al., 2001).

After participating in our Nyeri workshop, Michael Kibue, a Kenyan community development worker and social entrepreneur, took one idea from the workshop and ran with it. The idea was that complex issues *can* be tackled when you bring all the key actors around a table and you provide them with a step-by-step process to explore a problem. USAID uses a similar approach called 'System-wide Collaborative Action for Livelihoods and the Environment' (SCALE) where they bring all the major stakeholders to the table from the start (GreenCom, 2004). Michael brought together Masai herders and Nairobi butchers. They negotiated a new way of selling meat with fewer intermediaries. That was the start of the Livestock Stakeholder Self-help Association (Bekalo et al., 2002). Michael is

a social entrepreneur (later in the book we will refer to people like
him as a champion). He is familiar with the local context and is able
to broker new relationships. What I interpret in this example as
fitting with 'another development' was his lack of dependency on a
project package and its inevitable bureaucracy. Instead, he relied on
networks of trust and social capital he knew intimately. Once he had
established this foundation he did seek international development
funding, but on his own terms.

For the second example I cast my mind further back. In the early
1980s I worked for a small Colombian non-governmental organization. We built and operated several small farms where we tested and
demonstrated technologies with farmers. This was the heyday day
of the appropriate technology movement. We experimented with
water turbines, windmills, fishponds, biogas digesters, agroforestry,
composting and beekeeping. At one point, two farmers from Los
Encuentros, a community in the highlands of Antioquia, visited our
demonstration farm in San Luis. At their request we then travelled
together back to their community and helped them dig fishponds.
It did not take long for them to learn to build fishponds and handle
the fish. Some weeks later we returned for a visit and the same two
farmers had begun selling fingerlings to their neighbours. They had
also improved the draining system for the ponds and replaced the
plastic piles with locally available bamboo ones.

You will have noticed that both examples come from experience
working at a regional and local level. Little of this work has gone
to scale. While we could argue that both examples have elements
of Another Development, neither of them has led to structural
transformation. However, we feel they illustrate 'another' or 'good'
development because they show people making choices, investing and
finding rewards without logical frameworks and bureaucrats. They
are instances where people have been given the tools to express their
needs as they see them, participate in designing plans that they feel
they can handle, and carry out the plans at their own pace.

This is possible because communication is embedded in the process.
It is possible also because it relies on people's own initiative. The
reality is that most of the successful cases known to us have happened
without a dependency on a particular development project.

These have been instances where local people have seized an opportunity and engineered their own development. The very means by which the opportunities have been made possible have to do with an approach that 'searches' instead of imposing, that 'listens' first before telling.

Forgive us that all this has been said before. The sad fact is that one of the characteristics of the development industry is its unwillingness to learn from past mistakes – or even success. Or, conversely, from moments that have been successful. There is an insatiable desire to come up with something new without properly testing the old.

> People love something that is new. There is a disturbing but very real phenomenon of fashion in the development business. But you cannot be new forever. People will always look for something newer. You cannot retain the label of innovative 10 years after it was first applied to you. (Archer, 2007: 18)

The Kenyan and Colombian examples illustrate core principles from Another Development. In project jargon, there was no evident communication 'component' – beyond face-to-face communication, that is. Yet face-to-face happens to be the best communication method around. When it works, it is taken for granted. At the time, Ricardo prepared a booklet about tilapia fish production. It came in handy but mainly as a complement to the hands-on learning.

Had Don Snowden been there, we imagine that he would have said something along the lines that it was not the booklet that made this happen, nor the demonstration farm. They all contributed, but it was the farmers who get the credit. Their interest was matched with a relevant technology, and made available in a way that they could see, test and modify it. They could control and use it in their own terms – much like mobile phones, but we are getting ahead of ourselves.

Listeners lost ground to the tellers

In our understanding it is good development that breeds good communication. The 1980s were not ideal times. Yet, compared to today, the development context then provided windows of opportunity for experiments in participatory development. This was accompanied by development agencies that opened or expanded their communication units. In contrast, today much of the participatory excitement has been set aside. Aid organizations have closed their communication units or shifted them to fit their information and public-relations needs. Somehow the listeners lost ground to the tellers. In the next chapter we explain how this happened: the searchers lost ground to the planners. Today we have fewer briefcases like Paul's in pubs and more people looking at computer databases. Beyond the romantic notion, we argue that this shift was profound.

This was before development became what a colleague dubbed 'industrialized'. Agencies were willing to provide funds for innovation and experimentation. They allowed people to fail. And, as we all know, failure breeds learning. Now the fear of failure is so intense that they straitjacket innovation with tools and guidelines (logical frameworks, results-based management). These days all you have to do is get the paperwork right. Have you seen donor reports lately?

THREE

Planners and searchers:
two ways of doing development

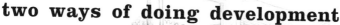

Communication is not the same as telling

Years ago the same colleague who produced the letter to the professor was putting together material for a workshop on Communication for Development. He wrote an introduction stating what should be obvious – that communication is not the same as telling. That simple thought seems to stick. We use it often to explain the difference between information (telling) and communication (both listening and telling). It is amazing how little that notion is understood, let alone applied, in the development business.

It is not that there is anything inherently wrong in 'telling' – it is just that it isn't communication. It tends to be the domain of people who feel they know what should be done: parents, school principals and, unfortunately more often than not, those in development. In contrast, Nora Quebral writes that communication is reciprocity of thought (Quebral, 2002).

Between the 1950s and the 1970s there was growth with attention to equity; since then there has been growth in its absence (Nederveen Pieterse, 2008). In the 1970s and 1980s we made note of those little pockets of both good development and good communication. The idea that things had to be done differently was relatively strong at the time.

The writings coming out of Latin America – Paulo Freire, Orlando Fals Borda, Juan Díaz Bordenave and Luis Ramiro Beltrán – had a strong influence on development thinking and communication. At the same time, Robert Chambers was beginning to introduce the world of participatory development. People were lining up to take courses in methods like Rapid Rural Appraisal (RRA) and Participatory Rural Appraisal (PRA). The notion of people-centred development was born. Now development has been taken over by the technocrats. The same could be said for communication. Earlier we paraphrased Silvio Waisbord's image of communication as playing second fiddle in the larger development field. Here is the full quotation:

> The fortunes of communication have been tied to the predomi-
> nance of a technical mindset that believes that economics, health
> or agricultural challenges only require economic, medical or
> agricultural expertise. The social sciences may be occasionally
> invited to play second fiddle under the watchful eye of the expert
> conductor or to produce 'flavour of the month' ideas. (Waisbord,
> 2007)

Now, however, in the second half of this decade, the information revolution has created a surge in interest in communication – what many call strategic communication. But this is mostly true when the term is associated with public relations, information, media – all about 'telling'. 'Listening', a key aspect of communication, is missing from the equation.

There is dissent. In the last two years we have joined several training workshops on alternative assessment and evaluation methods. We have been surrounded by development practitioners who were reaching the limits of their commitment. The heart and soul have seeped out of the development world. It has, without doubt, turned into a giant business governed at a corporate level with mind-numbing rules and regulations. Development aid agencies set the rules and large contractors get the business (Collier, 2007). The aid sector behaves like an industry leaving little room for creativity and innovation, a hallmark of good development.

This reality is particularly painful around the obsession to *measure success*. Wendy recently completed three exhausting weeks preparing project implementation plans for a non-governmental development organization that receives bilateral funding. Her team was required to figure out who would spend how much, when and on what in the year 2011. This in a project designated to improve the livelihoods of the ultra-poor and marginalized groups in the uncertain post-earthquake environment of Pakistan. They were underspent when last we spoke, notwithstanding the plan.

Planners and searchers

Many books have been written on the development theme. Unless you are a development junkie you won't read them. They are full of jargon and hard to follow. How did we come up with language so dense and complicated? Yes, development is messy and open to many interpretations. We get stuck on details; we respond by inventing new words. Others pick them up and overnight another trend is out. This phenomenon happens in many fields; however, in ours it is inexcusable. What we write is no longer understandable to the people we aim to help; it does not even make sense to the people we live with. Just ask our spouses, who roll their eyes at those moments when we are brave enough to tell them about what we are writing. If this sounds familiar, you will enjoy Chapter 4.

It can be quite refreshing to break this bad habit. We celebrate a few authors who have achieved this. Ricardo Gómez and Benjamín Casadiego wrote 'Letter to Aunt Ofelia' in an effort to make development ideas accessible to anyone, including Aunt Ofelia (Gómez and Casadiego, 2002). Paul Curtis Richards wrote his Ph.D. dissertation as a novel. We still remember his 'reasonable social scientist' as a character espousing the theories he most disliked (Richards, 1985). They inspired us. They made their work accessible to others.

Ricardo recalls the example of an outstanding communicator whose cartoons were part of his Mexican childhood.

A master of this art is Mexico's Eduardo del Rio, a political cartoonist who publishes under the pen name Rius. Rius is known throughout Latin America for his work. He has made this into his profession – I grew up with his work. His first book, *Cuba for Beginners* (1970) was so popular that it was translated into English. The titles of his books illustrate his witty humour. He uses cartoons to challenge dominant politics. His 2007 book entitled *Cómo acabar con el país (sin ayuda extranjera)* (*How to Destroy the Country without Foreign Aid*) criticizes the failed national attempts at stemming deforestation. His work is widely read. High schools use it to make Mexican development challenges accessible to the young, contradictions and all. I recall a drawing by Rius showing some bearded men in lab coats gliding in the sky. He called it 'the planners', making use of the double meaning of the word in Spanish: to plan and to glide. I could not find it, but I was able to contact him and explain why this image was so relevant to our book. To our surprise he produced another version for us...

It strikes me how effective his work has been and how it has not been part of the development industry – perhaps because it is home-grown?

Two recent books have tried to bring a touch of sanity back into the development business: *White Man's Burden* (Easterly, 2006) and *The Bottom Billion* (Collier, 2007). Both have been written by former employees of the World Bank who, after fairly long careers at the Bank, are now teaching development at universities. Both are economists who have decided to state their dissident views, which contrast sharply with those espoused by the Bank. And both are no doubt in their fifties or early sixties. We have a theory about that, but more on this later.

Collier presents a carefully constructed argument to support the notion that setting the conditions for economic growth is the only possible way out for the bottom billion. Easterly, on the other hand, takes a completely opposite tack arguing that there is no grand solution that can be applied to get people out of poverty. Instead, he argues, smaller, targeted initiatives, preferably defined by the people themselves, will eventually provide solutions bit by bit to confront the problems of poverty. No doubt both arguments have merit. Easterly presents ideas closely related to much of what we have said above and we have borrowed thoughts and ideas from his work.

Easterly divides the development world into 'planners' and 'searchers'. The 'planners', he maintains, think they can come up with the 'big plan' to end world poverty. In contrast to this, 'searchers' try to find small ideas that might actually work in pockets to alleviate a specific problem. Searchers, he maintains, will know if something works only if the people at the bottom can give feedback – that is why successful searchers have to be close to the customers at the bottom, rather than surveying the world from the top.

Conversely, 'planners' set the big goals. Setting goals, he agrees may be good for motivation but is counterproductive for implementation. The complexity of ground reality dooms any attempt to achieve the end of poverty through a plan, and no rich society has ended poverty in this way. Planners are accountable upwards. They are always looking over their shoulders back to the office at headquarters (promotion central) rather than forward to the ground at their feet. However, Easterly points out, the big plans at the top keep the rich people happy because 'something is being done'. But (and here is the caveat) if ineffective big plans take the pressure off the rich to help the poor, the tragedy is that then the effective piecemeal actions may not happen.

When Wendy was working for the Bank in Delhi she always felt that her boss was looking over his shoulder back to Washington – it was a distinct impression. She once asked him (when he was sitting behind a huge pile of reports almost hiding him from view) why he did this; he answered after a pause, 'For the poor I guess.'

Easterly believes acknowledging that development happens mainly through home-grown efforts would liberate the agencies of the West from utopian goals, freeing up development workers to concentrate on more modest, doable steps to make poor people's lives better. This succinctly brings us back to the theme of our book.

Searchers listen; planners tell

We think that Easterly would agree that those who favour 'telling' are the 'planners' of this world. After all, if you or your organization have come up with a big plan for eradicating poverty, the only thing you can do is tell people and governments how to stick to the rules so that the big plan will work. Isn't that how we end up with Structural Adjustment Programmes; Social Action Plans and now Poverty Reduction Strategic Plans?

We realize that what we were doing to explain the difference between 'tellers' and 'listeners' mirrored the Easterly idea of 'planners' and 'searchers'. It is a convenient way to identify a thought instantly. While we, like Easterly, understand that the world is not nicely divided into black and white, we have found that it helps to be polemical in order to explain our thinking.

Ricardo recently interviewed a man who had worked in Bolivia. He shared his frustration with the development industry; the use of logical frameworks to pretend one knows what will happen (when and how). He added that such tools will be difficult to replace. They are ideal for creating the illusion that you know what is going on without having to leave the comfort of your air-conditioned office. Wendy recently sat through a briefing on Sustainable Livelihoods. The entire presentation was devoted to the data collection system – a complicated diagram indicating increase in income. Where are the people? Wendy takes this thought further.

Ricardo came back from a workshop on Outcome Mapping (a planning and evaluation methodology) and showed me one of his squiggles. During one of the sessions he had done what he often does to present an idea – that is sketch out a drawing to illustrate a thought or concept to help make it concrete for the listener. In this one he had divided the world into two paradigms (see our figure). On one side (the left side) he placed the technocrats. These are the 'planners'. They are the people believing in the value of log frames, results-based management and all the other trappings of the development world. Technocrats believe it is possible to measure change in a linear manner. They are accountable upwards. They are mostly concerned with the disbursement of funds. They are apt to rely on products (other than process). In communication terms they would be 'tellers' rather than listeners. For them communication is about telling people what to do and about changing behaviour.

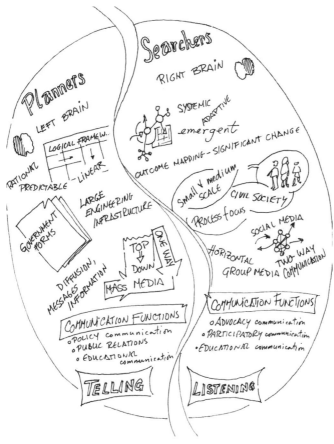

Did we tell you that we were going to be polemical?

On the right side we have the 'searchers'. Searchers think in terms of downward accountability and pay more attention to the actors and factors that contribute to a vision. They are satisfied if their projects contribute to good development without demonstrating direct attribution. Searchers tend to be process-oriented and in communication terms would be listeners (of course) rather than tellers. As 'listeners' they are more interested in participatory communication, advocacy and a search for common meaning.

Left-side, right-side thinking

Think about it. People are given tools to express their needs as they see them. That means that if people are encouraged to voice their own needs and are given the means to do so (radio forums; discussion groups; workshops; town councils), then someone else must be listening. If the listening is purposeful (in other words, if the tools were provided to enable the listening as well as the telling), then the response would be tailored to meet the expressed needs. Through dialogue and discussion a means would be found to respond to a development problem that would actually fit the aspirations and abilities of the people who need help. It should be simple. But of course it is not. Somehow the development business has grown into a bureaucratic nightmare that finds itself incapable of explaining itself even to those working in the field.

The left side of the brain gives us the logical, linear way of thinking. The right side provides language, intuition and art. Of course this brain split just happens to coincide with the popular idea of the right side of the brain being able to think outside the box.

Can a planner become a searcher? Under the right conditions it is possible. In fact we mention people in this book who were planners with an affinity for searching. In her best-selling book *Drawing on the Right Side of the Brain* (1979) Betty Edwards explains that anyone can learn how to draw. The trick is not so much the skill; it is really about learning how to see well enough to draw (Edwards, 1979).

For Easterly the 'searchers' are using their right brain to seek out an alternative approach while the 'planners' are still doing the same old left-brain big plans that consistently miss the mark. How has this happened? We think it is because of intent – they do want to find the big plan to eradicate malaria or HIV/AIDS but don't want to do much, if anything, to rock the boat in terms of political clout and power. In the planning mentality there is no mention of the fundamental (structural) transformation at the core of Another Development. Development has been turned, after all, into a powerful business fuelled by loans and interest rates. On top of that, many of the larger organizations are run like large corporations but laden with bureaucratic requirements because of their links to government. It is the organizational culture and the context within which people work that tend to shape the decision-making and approach.

Did we forget the media?

Most Communication for Development books start by telling you what you can do with rural radio, and where television has drawbacks, and about the wonders of information and communication technologies (ICTs). And yet, so far, we have not even begun to address the media. We began this book by telling you that for years and years we thought that any international development project would be greatly improved by building in a planned communication strategy. This, we realized, was true up to a point.

What was true? That communication can shift development from a top-down telling attitude to a bottom-up searching one. Take the following example: a massive drainage and irrigation project in Mexico supported by the World Bank. The first phase of the Integrated Rural Development Programme for the Tropical Wetlands, Mexico (PRODERITH I) had been a top-down, centrally planned initiative with little involvement by people in the field. The government officials installed drainage and irrigation infrastructure without engaging farmers in the process. As a result farmers never felt the project was theirs. They failed to maintain the infrastructure, a familiar story.

At the start of the second phase in 1977, the approach was modified to include a process of consultation. Video was used to listen to what people already knew and to what they needed, in their terms. Field staff helped rural communities analyse their situation, articulate their collective perception and propose solutions. The video-based planning methodology became an integral part of the process in the water sector in Mexico. We think of this as a way to use media for active listening. Through the years of PRODERITH II these experiences had a profound impact. The director general of the National Water Commission went on record to announce that the government of Mexico would never again build any infrastructure without first involving the intended beneficiaries (FAO, 1991), a bold statement for a government official.

The use of video for listening, however, gave way to the telling. During the 1990s the Mexican government and the World Bank ran with the liberalization and privatization agenda. When Ricardo visited the project, the communication units had been instructed to change gear. They were told to become businesslike and earn their income. To survive they had to focus on producing training packages to satisfy the market. The Food and Agriculture Organization of the United Nations published case studies about both phases (FAO, 1987, 1996). The protagonists on the ground documented the shift towards a top-down, telling approach (Martínez Ruiz et al., 2006). The space, the resources and the mindset for using media to listen had disappeared. The environment no longer sustained the approach.

Hence our attention shifts – from a recent emphasis on *the medium used in a listening and searching mode* – to the context. When we say that we have come to understand that we should be looking at this all the other way around, what we mean is we have come to realize that the context is about good development, one that breeds good communication.

Silvio Waisbord provides a similar analysis regarding aid bureaucracies. He underlines how all incentives and reward systems for staff inside agencies favour the telling, the left brain, the top-down approach to communication (Waisbord, 2008). He makes us think about the colleagues we know inside the large aid organizations. They carve out a space to act as 'searchers', but the pressure to conform with the 'planners' is relentless, especially as the latter hold the purse strings. They work in a context where the conditions are opposed to Another Development, something we have come to refer to as the 'grey zone'.

Later in the book we come back to the media and the methods. How can we not when mobile phones are creating communication opportunities we never dreamt of and when opportunities for collaboration and two-way communication are exploding over the Internet? Marshall McLuhan spoke of the global village in the 1960s, a time so long past that he still talked about the 'electric' media. McLuhan understood the media and made forecasts with astounding accuracy. He even published a book about the medium being the 'massage'. You read it right, the 'massage' – of course he also wrote about the media being the message (McLuhan, 1965).

> All media work us over completely. They are so pervasive in their personal, political, economic, aesthetic, psychological, moral,

ethical, and social consequences that they leave no part of us untouched, unaffected, unaltered. The medium is the massage. Any understanding of social and culture change is impossible without a knowledge of the way media work as environments. All media are extensions of some human faculty – psychic or physical. (McLuhan and Fiore, 1967: 26)

Father Roberge told Wendy when she visited him in Kolkata that we are like fish in the 'media water' and we only realize we are in it when we jump out temporarily. You are invited to jump out of the water with us for a few chapters. While we are up in the air, we will look back at decades of Communication for Development work. We will then plunge back in, better informed to make more realistic choices in our careers and profession. While we are there we need to be critical and learn from our own mistakes. We are doing this by hitting our softest spot: why is it that we are so useless at explaining what we do?

FOUR

Why communicators can't communicate

We are returning from a disastrous soccer tournament. Our boys managed to tie one game – the rest of the scores are best forgotten. Dave is driving the van full of smelly, demoralized teenagers. 'So what do you do?' asks Dave.

The best part of the soccer season is meeting the soccer dads and moms: you come across people in all sorts of professions. 'I work in development, also do some communication stuff.' He is quiet for a moment as if he lost his way. 'Like housing and condos?' he asks. 'Oh, no; not that kind of development, more like international projects, and I work up north with Aboriginal communities.'

A full half hour later I am running out of words to explain what I meant. He is politely nodding. Desperate to get out of this rut I ask back: 'And you Dave, what do you do?' His reply delivers the full meaning with two words: 'Fix cars.' A scant minute ago I thought of myself as a communication specialist.

I work in communication, but not the kind you think

When people ask us this question we tend to mumble something and find ourselves getting evasive. People would think we were hiding our profession – working for an intelligence agency perhaps, except that someone in that field would already have a firm answer. Sometimes we manage to get out the word 'communication' but then hastily add in 'but for development' and then the look of puzzlement makes us falter. Often we just stick to 'communication' and then say 'but not the kind you think' and that leads us into a longer description.

'Why is this?' we ask ourselves. Find a room of like-minded communication types and the talking is incessant. Like any profession there is a kind of shorthand – a 'group think' and level of understanding that nullifies the need for explanation. But get us outside of our 'group-speak' and we falter. We are not alone in this.

Wendy laughed on listening to two thirty-something communicators from a creative communication group when she visited Kolkata. While the group Thoughtshop takes on a range of communication initiatives, they tell their parents they are working in media and public relations. This, they say, is easier and allows the parents to nod with understanding and ask no further questions.

Of course it is not that anyone is hiding anything – it is just so difficult to explain. We have thought about this a lot and decided we would offer explanations. See what you think.

There is something fuzzy about a profession that includes the word 'communication'. For one thing the word itself means different things to different people. And the point is that, as a word, it definitely means something to everyone. We imagine it would be easier to be an astrophysicist or any profession equally opaque. Ask them what they do and the conversation stops right there unless you have a good joke. Ask us, and we are torn between letting the general understanding of communication ride or getting into one of those conversations that go around the block, like the previous chapters.

Apparently even people who are working in media and communication have the same problem (that pesky word 'communication'). We include a quotation from a book written by a woman who took the pilgrimage on the Camino de Compostela in Spain. She describes her various conversations with fellow pilgrims. Here is the one that caught our attention:

> 'So what is it that you actually do?' Kate asked me… It was a good question. I had been in my job for two years, and I still couldn't articulate what it involved or describe the raison d'être of the organization for which I worked. Whenever someone

asked me that question, I would stammer in confusion. This is
not a good sign when your title is manager of communications.
(Christmas, 2007: 88)

Oh how we understand. At a gathering in Kabul recently, Wendy
casually asked someone what he was doing. You know how it is – who
are you with, what is your job, where do you work? He mumbled
an answer and said that his work was sort of vague. Immediately
she wondered, could he be one of us? No doubt against his will,
she kept on asking until he confessed that he worked in 'strategic
communications'. They did have a good laugh. But even then they
had their share of differences in describing to each other what it
is that they actually do. They spoke the same language but with a
different accent.

Silvio Waisbord captures this when he writes: 'For better or worse,
communication is rather a catchall category, conceptually complex
and flexible, whose ambiguity is impossible to resolve despite several
cogent efforts to put old debates to rest' (Waisbord, 2007). The
'conceptual confusion' that Waisbord is talking about was apparent
in Wendy's conversation with the same man in Kabul later on in
the evening. She got the sense that his particular view of 'strategic
communication' was focused on helping governments (or the military)
strategically use communication to get their point across – telling
people what they wanted them to do or hear. There is nothing wrong
with this, but it is not the kind of communication that we are talking
about in this book.

I fix cars, I make posters, I produce videos

Waisbord is categorical: communication and information are not the
same. There is a substantial difference, he explains, between sending
information in different formats, and people exchanging ideas and
values. We agree, and we are not alone; Fuglesang presents this
clearly:

Information is not communication. Information is only potential
communication. We must use information in the right way, in the
right social context. Communication between people thrives not
on the ability to talk fast, as some mass-media prophets seem to

think, but on the ability to listen well. We do not communicate by cramming an enormous quantity of 'information bits' together into a monologue, but by being socially intelligent and capable of listening to what the other person has in mind before we respond. It is so simple, and yet we fail continuously in our attempt to communicate because of an egocentric attitude. (Fuglesang, 1982: 28)

We also agree with Waisbord when he notes that if we make community dialogue and participation the litmus test for bona fide communication, we quickly run out of work. Oh yes; nevertheless it is the communication that promotes community dialogue and participation that stands at the centre of this book. That is because we firmly believe this is the linchpin of what makes communication such an integral part of development. It is also what makes it so difficult to explain concretely. 'I fix cars.'

> In bureaucracies where power and prestige are anchored in strict professional criteria (e.g. educational credentials, career paths), communication is generally perceived as another 'service' unit. It is seen as either a 'soft science' that fails the tests of modern scientific knowledge (sound methodologies? predictability? hard facts?). It is often called an 'art,' one of the worst insults that can be hurled in institutions that uphold 'the scientific model.' (It should also be admitted that 'art' is actually a badge of honour for communication staff who believe that their job, indeed, is an art.) Besides, who cares for science when posters and press releases are needed? Can't anybody come up with a catchy slogan with a clever rhyme? (Waisbord, 2007)

This brings us to the old 'product' versus 'process' discussion. It is much easier to explain a concrete product (I fix cars, I make posters, I produce videos) than to explain a process (I give tools to people so they can talk to each other – oh really?). No doubt we would be much better off telling a story to illustrate how communication for development might work. Usually people have wandered off when you get to that point.

Of course when we really need people to understand (like decision-makers, for example), then we pull out all stops – but even then we are not always successful. Take the basic notion of audience research. Wendy remembers working briefly for a World Bank mission in Uganda:

The project was all about promoting a Nile Basin agreement calling for all nine countries in the Nile Basin to share water rights. The task manager was very energetic and determined to see this through. He wanted a communication strategy that would 'get the message out' as soon as possible. I told him that we couldn't just do that immediately without some basic audience research to understand the context. 'What', he said, 'what are you talking about – we already know the message.' 'But', I said, 'this message will mean different things to different people – a person from Sudan will not hear the message the same way that a person from Egypt will hear it.' I never went back to this project so I don't know what happened. I do know there was a lot of talk about participation, but old-style, retired water engineers were asked back to head the teams for each individual country.

It was not the only time this happened. For example, I think back to the time I set up a small communication component for a large (very large) multi-donor irrigation project in Pakistan. CIDA was a minor donor managing a socio-economic study. I had a small fund which I was able to spend on a communication initiative. This made it possible to contract two consultants with strong credentials in participatory video. Familiar with Don Snowden and the Fogo Process (described in Chapter 6), we felt that it would be useful to work with video to interview farmers and families living within the reach of the irrigation project to ask them how the project might affect their lives. The intention was to find a way to let the Pakistani Engineering Authority and the World Bank hear the views of the poorer farmers living along the system (the project was located in an area of Pakistan still feudal in culture, with large landowners and tenant farmers). I went to great pains to explain the purpose of the video both to the Bank and to the government. After the videos were produced and were shown to the authorities there was a substantial backlash. What the Bank and the Engineering Authority had expected to view was a public relations documentary extolling the virtues of the project. What they got were the voices of small farmers worrying about the effects of salinity on their crops. Even though I had explained what I would be doing and why (participatory communication), the Bank and the water authorities heard something different (public relations). It was a stand-off.

For months after that I was shunned by both groups – years later I still felt fearful of bumping into the Bank engineers in the corridors in Washington. Much later in Pakistan I did meet up with one of the Bank task managers. He laughed when I told him my fears and said that now the Bank uses video all the time. I wonder how they are using it?

Right-brainers in a left-brain world

In Mozambique we had a similar experience. Try as we might, we could not seem to find success in explaining basic notions of communication planning to the heads of different government water departments. We drew pictures, we sat together one-on-one in lunchtime meetings and we told stories. We just could not explain it properly. It wasn't until some government employees went to the field with Ricardo to actually participate in an audience research exercise that the whole notion of 'process' became apparent.

Don't get us wrong, we don't think it is 'them' who are always at fault; it is our inability to put into words a concept that often eludes us. Where is the metaphor to make it stick?

One of Wendy's sons used to work in software development. He has no trouble understanding this problem because he experienced the same thing himself. He said that no matter how hard he and his colleagues tried to get the point across that software had to be designed through consultation with the intended user, the engineers would present the idea and tell them to make it work. This sounds familiar to us. Planners know and do not hesitate to tell. For them listening is off the radar; why bother to listen when you already believe you know the answer? Enter the right-brain searchers who talk about first finding out what the client wants and needs – and you have trouble. We are worlds apart.

In Chapter 3, we spoke about the left-brain versus right-brain discussion. We described how we felt that 'communication for development' is really a right-brain function trying to make it in a left-brain world. While it is true that we take a somewhat 'tongue in cheek' approach to this comment, we think there is some truth to what we say. In her 2008 book, *My Stroke of Insight*, the neuroanatomist

Jill Bolte Taylor describes in vivid terms how her stroke helped her gain new insight into the two sides of the human brain. We live in a left-side world, she explains. That's how we are rewarded in our society: for training our left hemispheres to perform better, to learn more details, to become specialists in our area of expertise. That, she says, is all left hemisphere. It's all push. It's judgmental. The right brain, on the other hand, is a time when we pause. It is more sympathetic rather than judgmental – it can be lost in the moment (Bolte Taylor, 2008).

Now you don't really want to be going around at gatherings explaining how communication for development is a right-brained activity. We doubt that would win anyone over. The idea, however, does make you think. In fact, finding the right words and the right tone to explain the thinking behind communication for development is difficult. Wendy's son argues that we should get rid of the word 'communication' altogether. He says that it has such a strong meaning for so many people that the word itself misleads. It is impossible for people to escape from the idea of information, media and public relations (all tools of extreme importance in a corporate world).

We guess that is why it is such a relief to talk to like-minded people; every profession shares this thought. A few months ago Wendy was talking to Chris Morry from the Communication Initiative, a network that promotes this field. She happened to be in Victoria, Canada, where the Communication Initiative is based and sought him out to talk about ideas. Over coffee Chris started telling her about his work with the Global Polio Eradication Initiative. At one point he said that of course we aren't always doing 'good' communication and carried on talking, *knowing* that she would know what he meant. This insider understanding may be comfortable – like families with their own codes for shared experiences – but we still need to explain our work to the wider world.

For over five years in the early 1980s Ricardo enjoyed cappuccinos with a view to the Forum – the best of Rome. He describes how he worked with a dozen fun-loving, critical and creative people. When he first arrived, the Development Support Communication group of FAO felt like a non-governmental organization. That is, as long as the door was shut. Open the door and the group were in the business of carving space for communication inside the endless meeting rooms and straight-angled, marbled halls of FAO.

Ricardo says he can still feel it: off to another to meeting to sell communication (should he wear a tie?). In an earlier job he had vaccinated goats, planted leucaena trees, built tilapia fish ponds with farmers. Now he was facing specialists in each subject area while he was the one wearing the communication hat. Once all the meaty content had been discussed they would to turn to him:

> 'We need a video about fertilizers for the Andes.'
>
> 'OK, I see. And if I may ask: Why a video? Who is it for? What do they already know? How do they already exchange information about farming?'
>
> 'Sorry, we don't have the budget for all of that.'

Back then he would return to his team and lament about how little these specialists understood what communication was all about. Today he recognizes it as a paradox: in our own field of communication we fail to reach our audience.

The late Colin Fraser, who used to head Ricardo's former unit at FAO, often said that those of us in Communication are terrible at describing what we do. We clearly agree. In addition, we have not been clear to ourselves. For a long time those of us who belong to this cult of communication practitioners have believed that good communication makes good development. When we say good communication we are talking about participatory communication; one that emphasizes 'listening' instead of mainstream communication that focuses on 'telling'. When we say 'good development' we mean that people are given the tools to design, discuss and implement their own development.

We think of participatory communication as one that shapes the very nature of development. We think of conventional communication as the one that simply promotes the desired development outcome.

PART II

What we learned

FIVE

Working in the grey zone

There are a few good development situations where communication shines – and many extremely bad ones – but most of the time we are working somewhere in the middle. Here the conditions are never right and we often wonder where we are going and why, but keep on trying – that is why we call it the grey zone. In this chapter we share what we have learned about working in this area. Often it feels like navigating an obstacle course: clarifying what is being asked of us, understanding the conditions we work in, and on that basis adjusting our expectations and our communication methodologies. Writing this book has been an exercise in reflection. We have shifted our attention away from methodology onto the conditions where we work.

We have come to realize that there are three factors that help us navigate in the grey zone: the champions, the context and the different communication functions. These three factors make up our framework. Throughout this book we explain what we mean by this, but first we want to tell you some stories from our work in the grey zone. Ricardo begins with a story from the darker side of the zone. He lived through this experience some years back when he joined a project formulation mission for a multilateral development agency. The job was to prepare a project proposal for a regional rural development project. It could just as easily happen today.

All that was left was a two-way car radio

We were an assembly of specialists from every conceivable field of international development. For once, a communication component was being designed from the very beginning of a large rural development project in Nepal. And I was part of the crowd. I came with plenty of examples of good practice; this time it was going to work.

A dozen of the other subject matter experts came to me asking to have communication activities built into their component. The project depended on communication for capacity development, for engaging rural households in deciding on priorities, for advising communities about new policies, and to get feedback from beneficiaries in remote villages.

I recall having tea with a lot of government officials – the higher up the colder the office. I felt like one more of what Easterly (2002) calls 'the cartel of good intentions', banging at their door with yet another proposal. When did the officials ever find time to get their own work done… how many visitors like me must they see every week?

I visited the remote western region of Nepal where the project was to be based. I met with community leaders and local organizations. I gained a sense of the needs and of existing skills. I priced out local equipment and personnel. I even found some Kathmandu-based Communication for Development specialists who had worked with Joe Ascroft. Ascroft was a professor of communication in Ohio who had managed an FAO project that I had supported when I was in Rome. I was on a roll.

Yet when I met with NGOs (non-governmental organizations) they were sceptical. Such multimillion-dollar loans tended to stay in government. NGOs were not wanted. Oh but this time it was going to be different, I assured them. There would be a role for them. Little by little I started to feel uneasy. I voiced my fear to the head of the mission. Most of us on the mission were convinced that NGOs had to be involved in the implementation but the government would not allow that. To me it looked like an impasse, but not to him. 'Why, then, would the government ever approve the project?' I asked. 'Oh they will sign it alright', he said; 'if they don't sign this one they won't get the other. And that one they really want.'

One day at lunchtime I noticed that the mood had changed. The mission leader was nervous. One of the donors that had contributed grant money to lessen the burden of the loan had pulled out. 'Why?' I asked. 'Don't ask – some directive from head office.' The goalposts had shifted and the number cruncher on the mission was redoing the tables. The rest of us were told to reduce our budgets. The hesitating voices from the NGOs came back to haunt me as I struggled to revise my logical framework and budget. My own doubts, the ones I had been convincing myself to ignore, grew back.

Months later I bumped into one of the leaders of the formulation team. I asked about 'my' communication component. Without hesitation he mentioned that the Appraisal Mission (a team of economists who put things into smaller boxes) had cut it out. What was left? A two-way car radio for the vehicle.

With the money spent on my fees and travel several of those NGOs could have worked for over a year. What was I thinking? Welcome to navigating in the grey zone.

What happened here? Donors mostly pay lip service to the idea of participation. Because of this Ricardo got invited to join the formulation mission. He accepted with alacrity. Rarely is communication invited into a project from the beginning. However, the context turned out to be all wrong. The multilateral to government loan environment rarely allows NGOs into the implementation mix – and this is where much of the communication know-how resides. As soon as there are limitations to funding, the communication component is the first to go.

If you are a communication practitioner you will be able to relate to this story. What could have saved the situation? The presence of a champion within government or the multilateral donor agency could make a difference. Take James Grant for example.

James Grant was the iconic director of UNICEF for fifteen years (1980–95). He made UNICEF a leader in communication during his tenure. How? He personified communication in his every action. He believed in its importance and he understood its impact. When he travelled he carried a packet of oral rehydration therapy solution in his pocket. When he met with prime ministers or other leaders he would pull out the packet and say, 'do you know that this costs less than a cup of tea and it can save hundreds of thousands of children's lives in your country?' (Heath and Heath, 2007, 125) Heath and Heath underline that Grant was a man who made ideas stick. Had UNICEF under Grant been present in Ricardo's formulation mission, communication would not have been so easily dropped.

In Chapter 2 we described how Communication for Development lost its position over the last two decades. As practitioners we pleaded for any kind of communication input into development planning – we sought the crumbs. On the rare occasion that we got invited to join formulation missions for large projects, it seemed to us as if a window had opened – we jumped to take advantage of the moment. We saw these windows as moments for policy influence (Lindquist, 2001). And yet, most often, just as in the Nepal example, these moments evaporated when the planners moved in.

While Ricardo worked directly as a communication officer at the Food and Agriculture Organization of the United Nations in Rome, Wendy tried something different. She went to work as a generalist for CIDA. She was posted to Ghana and managed the CIDA investment in water and sanitation there. Later she went to Pakistan to cover irrigation and drainage. She tried to become as knowledgeable as possible within these fields. As she explains below, her plan was to use this window to bring communication in through the back door.

When I look back I see I was somewhat smug about this. I had my comeuppance when I worked as a community development and communication specialist for the World Bank Regional Water and Sanitation Group in New Delhi. This was a dismal failure. I spent a lot of time networking and talking about process – my boss wanted communication products (where are the posters?). I wasn't experienced enough to articulate where I was going with communication. I was in the wrong place at the wrong time – I was a woman among a team of male achievers. I was a communication person and not an engineer. Water and sanitation was still the domain of engineers. I was a complete outsider to the Bank culture.

Even though Wendy felt ineffective in that particular place and time, the idea of being placed within a sectoral initiative was a sound one. Carefully planned communication should be central to any development initiative – who best to support this than someone familiar with the various issues germane to the sector?

We return to the PRODERITH example from Mexico introduced in Chapter 3. The Mexican example has become a popular case study (Fraser, 1987; FAO, 1996). It is noteworthy that a large governmental system was able to experiment with new approaches; in essence, an innovation that created a precedent at a national scale. We have used the PRODERITH experience worldwide. At times we wonder whether we have promoted it too much. We recently interviewed some of the protagonists in this experience. They confirmed that the conditions that enabled this searching and listening to happen are no longer present (Martínez Ruiz et al., 2006). The telling side of communication came back to dominate. The exciting phase ended. Yet we have promoted it broadly as if it were still alive. We have now come to think that these experiences are much like orchids.

Orchid collections

On the good side of the grey zone there are worthy projects, organizations and moments where communication shines. PRODERITH was one such example. Many of these are captured in collections of success stories; *Communication: A Key to Human Development* (FAO, 1994) and *Making Waves*, by Alfonso Gumucio-Dagron (2001) are good examples. We explain the essence of these stories through an analogy. The orchid is a beautiful flower that only blooms now and again and only when the conditions are right. We tend to make reference to famous communication projects as if they were showcase orchids. Yet we forget to explain that today the flower is no longer on the stalk. We do not take notice of the conditions that made it bloom in the first place.

Think about it: when the conditions are not there, the plant sits for a long time doing nothing exceptional – with the potential hidden within. In this book we share several prize 'orchids', but more often we draw attention to the conditions that enabled them to bloom. When we talk about conditions, many dimensions come to mind: the politics of the day, the institutions, the culture and history, the patterns of media control and funding. Context is like a soup where the media, the norms and our actions are all interrelated. Father Roberge has spent his life explaining the impact of media on people's lives. In the next chapter we explore why he says that the media are the air we breathe. While we agree with this notion, one that is comparable to McLuhan's, we view context in a wider sense to include history, geography and culture.

The fact that projects, like orchids, may have a short-lived exuberance is not surprising. This is part of life. Organizations, like organisms and ecosystems, go through cycles. In international development there is a fascination with best practices and replication. If a pilot project goes well, we make it into a cookie cutter and try to scale it up. Except in the real world this fails because the nature of the beast is not the same. The intense, creative force behind each new initiative is different from the task of multiplication. So, instead, in this book we extract from every success story the elements or conditions that made it work in the first place. We think of them as coordinates for navigation. You don't transplant an orchid from one environment to another. You find a local variety and a good gardener, and the right soil. You use the type of watering, light and temperature regime that worked in one place, and you experiment with a local variation.

Enough botany. So what is it we can do to navigate in the grey zone? We mentioned the three coordinates that guide our actions: champions, context and the ability to choose different communication functions for each initiative.

If this sounds basic and straightforward to you, good for you! It took us twenty-five years to figure it out.

Three coordinates for navigation

Champions are individuals or organizations with a sincere respect for the views of the people with whom they work and with people's ability to solve many of their own problems. They follow the principles of Another Development. They are Freirean in their outlook. Like the Brazilian educator and activist Paulo Freire, they have a sincere belief in helping people discover their own potential. To them it is clear that any progress depends on people becoming aware of the causes behind their situation, and acting to overcome them. Champions are the rarest among the three components. They are hard to find, they cannot be replicated, and yet their presence has often been the key to making something that might have been humdrum into a successful initiative. As practitioners, we have been able to play the role of champions only for short moments. But mostly we have not.

The second coordinate is context. Context has to do with communities, geography, culture and history. Context is also about the organizations, donor institutions and corporations that shape the economy of a community. It includes government, politics, policies and funding rules, packaged into projects. Context also includes the media that shape how we think, perceive and contribute or not to transform our predicament. Our focus is on achieving an understanding of the many dimensions of a context or environment. Time matters: champions who stay in one place are immersed in the context. They are familiar with the nuances, they know the situation, they have developed trust within their environment and they are able to act when the time is right. If you have a champion in context for a long time, you have the two most important components in place.

The third coordinate is about communication. We have found it effective to talk about what communication is for, rather then spend much time on definitions (Ramírez and Quarry, 2004a). Here we refer to the fact that a communication initiative may require a wide variety of functions depending on the intended purpose of the intervention. As we noted in Chapter 1, these tend to fall along a continuum from direct *telling* (public relations and technology transfer) to a mix of both *telling* and *listening* to effect predetermined change (social marketing and behavioural change) to a focus on *listening, exchange* and *dialogue* (advocacy and participatory). We well understand that each one of these functions fulfils important felt needs. We have trouble with the fact that the development industry favours the left side of the continuum (telling) when so often situations require a right-side approach (listening). Our bias in favour of the listening ones is rooted in their affinity with Another Development.

Ricardo came up with the case of Radyo Tucunan, an orchid that bloomed for some time. This case was part of an FAO project to improve communication in agriculture in five regions of the Philippines. We use it to illustrate the coordinates of Communication for Another Development. Several communication advisers were in place during the implementation of the project. Two were committed to developing a farmer-first approach. They believed in the potential of participatory communication. The project leaders in the Philippines government organization were equally committed. In Region 9 on the west of Mindanao, the regional coordinator was a firm believer in a participatory approach. This collection of champions allowed for a real engagement with the farm communities in Tucunan. Radyo Tucunan stands out because it kept going years after the project ended.

The project started with the farmers. This followed the tradition of participatory rural appraisal that was popular at the time. The project team asked farmers to identify the most urgent needs in farming. They were also asked to propose what media combination they would want to use to learn more about those very needs. In Tucunan they opted for community audio towers – an idea borrowed from Thailand where loudspeakers are placed across the village. They then organized and installed a small broadcast unit. Radyo Tucunan broadcast the 'school on the air' every morning. The rest of the day the radio was busy with other programming of interest to the community. For once the project measured the change brought about by the communication effort and FAO published a case study showing the changes in adoption (FAO, 1995).

Years later at a gathering in the Netherlands, Ricardo bumped into a colleague who still worked with the government agency that had coordinated the project. She reported that Radyo Tucunan was still operational, all funding coming from the community. Clearly the community was the champion in context. The communication process started with *participatory functions*: listening to what mattered to farmers and asking them to select the media and schedule that fitted their needs. Next came *educational communication* through the training programmes they called 'school on the air'. The educational programmes had been effective, new practices were adopted and yields increased. She reported, however, that life for those communities remained difficult. The success with rice yields led to an increase in the price of the lands they rented. We were far from shifting structures, a core principle of Another Development.

A primer on communication functions

Some time back, a paper on communication for sustainable development by Niels Röling from Wageningen caught our attention (Röling, 1994). Niels has always been a critical thinker about communication; he suggested that the field of communication for natural resource management could be split along three different functions.

Policy communication was about making rules known. It was about making policies known and relevant. Governments and large development agencies use this function on a regular basis.

The second function was *communication for sharing knowledge*. This included explaining biophysical information, such as the case of conventional transfer of technology efforts where farmers are given new tools or seeds to adopt. We refer to this as *educational communication*. Within this function there are variations: on the one hand there are participatory learning approaches where people come to understand the causes of a problem; on the other there are marketing approaches that seek short-term behaviour change. In the health field this function is used to promote the adoption of medical treatments, such as the case of the polio vaccine. Social marketing and other behaviour-change approaches are included in this function.

Röling then added *participatory communication*: giving a voice to different stakeholders to negotiate complex issues, such as the management of a watershed where no single party can have a solution that works for the others. This function makes use of group methods and techniques from the field of participation, from collaboration and from conflict management. Participatory communication methods and media are used to listen, to give a voice to those who are rarely heard.

We have added a complementary function: *advocacy communication*. That is what many organizations and social movements do when lobbying for changes in policies. Advocacy communication is the main function behind global campaigns promoted by civil society. Advocacy and participatory communication used to rely on traditional or group media (radio and video). Today we are all harnessing new tools, especially mobile phones and social networking though the Internet.

We have recognized that *organizational communication* is important for coordination purposes. In addition, we acknowledge *public relations.* We know that many organizations rely on this for fundraising. We also know that for large agencies and for corporations, it is synonymous with the term 'communication' (Quarry and Ramírez, 2005).

Participatory and advocacy communication are central for the champions and community-based organizations that work with the poor. These functions emphasize horizontal and bottom-up flows of information. They use media that can be locally controlled. They are increasingly utilizing new media to expand their lobbying efforts (Rheingold, 2002). Champions who work along these functions are active listeners; they are searchers.

Large development agencies, governments and multinational corporations are more comfortable with policy communication, educational communication and public relations. These are all *telling* approaches that planners expect to control. Röling voiced some optimism about shifts away from the top-down flow of information, and indeed new technologies are making this possible. Yet, overall, their appeal in the eyes of the development industry is their unidirectional and controlled pattern of information dissemination.

Working in the grey zone in Mozambique: an illustration of the coordinates

The project that we both worked on in Mozambique provides another case to illustrate the grey zone. The project focused on the institutionalization of a new national water policy that effectively introduced the World Bank's demand-based approach into the rural water sector. We were familiar with the Bank's push to privatize rural services. We had our doubts. Twice we had opted out of bidding for communication contracts in this field. However, in the case of Mozambique we dived into the grey zone, though not without hesitation. One reason for doing this was that Wendy had momentarily played the role of a champion. Wendy picks up the story.

In 1995 I was working with a private consulting firm. The firm was invited to Mozambique to participate in a study on institutional arrangements for managing the country's National Water Policy

(NWP). I was sent as one of three members for the task. During the mission I shared an apartment in downtown Maputo with two water engineers. We used the apartment as an unofficial office, setting up flip-charts and whiteboards in the living room. We had an abundant supply of cold beer in the fridge and often invited our government colleagues for a social evening after work. We would sit around the apartment and argue policy and ideas.

One colleague dropped by on a regular basis. One day we came back to find that he had been there and left scribbled diagrams on the flip-chart. Suddenly I realized that this informal exchange was far more important than the usual formal meetings and workshops that made up the sum total of our daily work. This led to our (Ricardo's and my) future involvement in the first stages of developing a communication strategy for the National Water Policy.

Wendy in the apartment was the champion-in-context, albeit compressed. She recognized the magnitude of the challenge. The government of Mozambique and the World Bank were switching to a demand-based approach in public services. Rural communities that grew up under a socialist regime were to become clients; they had to organize and register requests. Such requests would be channelled into competitive tenders. Water-drilling companies that had been doing business through networks of patronage now had to become competitive bidders for the contracts. The local and district governments had to become arbitrators in this new market for water drilling. This called for an unprecedented, collective change in the way of doing everything. Many communication functions would be appropriate; certainly policy and educational communication would be necessary.

We joined a team with two Maputo-based consulting firms and bid for the communication strategy that would help make this transition possible. We felt satisfied with our local partners. Ricardo was bringing some comparable experiences from Uganda. We knew the methods and *this time we were going to get it right.* Have you heard this one before?

The communication requirements were multiple. The Rural Water Transition Plan called for raising general awareness about the National Water Policy to increase its acceptance. We were to disseminate information on the application process and criteria for selection in districts selected for project inputs. In our mind this meant *policy communication*. Add to that the need to facilitate communication between communities, local authorities, water committees, district and provincial authorities. This, to us, was clearly about *organizational communication*.

There was plenty of talk about people's participation throughout the project; about collecting community contributions, reporting on status of water source, costs of repair, state of funds, and promoting good practices (Ramírez and Quarry, 2004b). While our thoughts would have naturally gone to *participatory communication*, we knew that this might be problematical for the Bank and the government. Doing the other two functions well was a tall enough order – especially as it was hard to find a champion among our local counterparts.

Our efforts were short-lived. While we eventually produced and pre-tested a suite of communication materials, our communication strategy stalled. Now we know why: we were missing a champion in context. Even though our team included two local consulting firms, they were outsiders. There was nobody staying on – inside – with a commitment to the principles of Another Development. There was no champion making sure local communities stayed involved. There was no one searching and listening. As we think back about this experience we realize how far off target we were from the beginning: just as Ricardo's experience in Nepal.

We use the three coordinates to understand the best cases, the orchids. We use them to decide what to do as communication practitioners. They help us navigate in the grey zone by giving us clues about what is possible or not. They help us gauge our expectations and adjust our approach.

The global context is mired with growing inequality, environmental threats and increasing tension. We find the development industry increasingly absurd. When we consider this broad context, when we look back at our experiences working in the grey zone, we conclude that Communication for Another Development badly needs more of the advocacy and participatory functions.

It may seem that we are creating a paradox. We state clearly that it is good development that is the prerequisite for good communication and not the other way around. This contradicts the years of struggle to convince decision-makers to include communication in development work. Decision-makers are happy with communication so long as it encompasses the functions on the left side of the continuum: policy and organizational communication, technology transfer and behavioural change. This communication may improve development but it will not change it. Advocacy and participatory communication are needed for that.

The champions know that. They have some sort of communication common sense (Quarry and Ramírez, 2008). They know what can be done, when and how. When they can, they embrace these functions because they sense that they are tools to modify the context. At the same time, if they stay in context and insist on applying the principles of Another Development, they are already creating the conditions for good development.

SIX

Early champions: uncovering principles

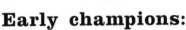

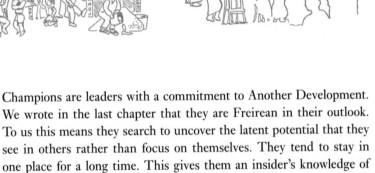

Champions are leaders with a commitment to Another Development. We wrote in the last chapter that they are Freirean in their outlook. To us this means they search to uncover the latent potential that they see in others rather than focus on themselves. They tend to stay in one place for a long time. This gives them an insider's knowledge of context. They either have a communication instinct or they bring in those who know the methods and media. They follow the participatory principles of Another Development (Dunn et al., 2007).

We have a sampling of individuals and organizations that fit this description. Each of them used the media in support of adult education and community development. We begin with those who experimented with new ways to use established media – film, photography, radio. In Chapter 7 we will show how these earlier experimentations have travelled – new people adapting new methods to new tools and newer challenges.

All but two in this first collection are people we knew or worked with, however briefly. Wendy shares her interviews with Don Snowden, the Canadian who pioneered the use of film and video for community empowerment. They worked together in Bangladesh. Next, she describes the work of Kolkata's Father Roberge, who, decades ago, trained local people to photograph positive images of life in the slums. She has met him several times both in India and in Canada and visited him again while writing this book. Ricardo highlights other champions: Alex Sim, who pioneered the Farm Radio Forum in Canada and whom he met just weeks before he died; and Manuel Calvelo-Rios and his work with pedagogical video in Peru.

In the next chapter we come to Alex and Wilna Quarmyne, promoters of community radio in Ghana; the Drishti team of video activists in Ahmedabad; Brian Beaton and the K-Net team of Internet champions for remote Aboriginal communities. We introduce you to Minou Fugelsang, HIV/AIDS activist in Tanzania, who is, in her own words, 'standing on Andreas's shoulders' to carry on some of his ideas.

This list is by necessity incomplete and biased towards the people we know. As you read, you will think of other names connected to your own life history. We realize there are many, and this book is but a small celebration of some of them and their achievements. We believe they would all agree that their achievement has to do with people taking control over their own destiny. They would credit neither themselves nor the media. That would be their hallmark.

The Fogo Process: a prize orchid

In Chapter 5 we introduced you to the Fogo Process – an experiment where film was used as a tool to enhance community development. Peter Lewis, a British communicator who made a study of this genre (1977), acknowledged what he called 'the worldwide debt to the Fogo Process', which, he wrote, fired enthusiasm in Europe and elsewhere in countries as far apart as Tunisia, Peru and Tanzania (Quarry, 1994).

> Paternity can be traced back to Fogo, as to an archetypal manuscript which spelt out for the first time the role reversal whereby those who had formerly been the 'object audience' became 'subject participants' in the message. To control the message is to enjoy power, an unusual enough experience for most of those involved, and one which generates the self-confidence that goes beyond media and encourages people to attempt the control of their lives as a whole. (Lewis, 1977: 2)

We learned that Mario Bravo, a Mexican communicator, was himself inspired by Fogo and experimented with the process in his country.

In the mid-1960s, Don Snowden was the head of the Extension Department at Memorial University. He and his team were working with remote fishing communities along the coast of Newfoundland and Labrador and the islands. The Trans Canada highway had only connected Newfoundland to the mainland in 1965. Television had just come to the islands, but most communication took place through coastal boats and word of mouth.

At this time, the government of Canada was putting together a report on poverty. As is so often the case, the people writing the report knew very little of the condition themselves; they presented some images that enraged Don Snowden. Simultaneously, Canada's National Film Board was preparing a series of films on rural poverty in the country. They chose Newfoundland for one of their locations. Don, who felt he definitely had something to say on the issue, met with the film-maker Colin Low and suggested they focus on Fogo Island. Snowden saw that the place illustrated the isolation and lack of organization and information that for him were clear indicators of poverty.

Fogo Island is 18 kilometres off Newfoundland's north-east corner. It is the most easterly point of North America. Fogo in the late 1960s was going through an economic crisis. Dependent on the fishing industry throughout its 300-year history, the inshore fishery had gradually dropped off, and Fogo fishermen were not equipped with long liners for offshore fishing. Over half of the male population was forced to go on welfare. Consequently the Newfoundland government, under premier Joey Smallwood had decided to move all outpost communities to resettle in more economically viable parts of the province. This meant the mainland.

Fogo Islanders did not want to move. A few people on Fogo set aside what Snowden would call 'their parochial concerns' to get together to form The Fogo Island Improvement Committee to seek ways to salvage the island way of life. Consequently Snowden accompanied Colin Low to the island so that he and one of his extension workers, Fred Earle, could personally introduce the idea of a documentary to the Fogo Island Improvement Committee. Colin Low would later explain: 'This project was to be more than the making of a film or films. Its purpose was to use film to assist a community to come to grips with some of its problems' (Nemtin and Low, 1972: 1).

At first Low planned to use a relatively conventional documentary approach by centring the film on the issue of resettlement. Gradually, however, a process began to evolve and the method changed radically. Low decided to focus on personalities rather than problems. He discovered the ease with which people were interviewed in their own milieu and realized how vibrantly they spoke, telling their stories to illustrate the strengths and weaknesses of life on Fogo.

> I was surprised by how readily people were prepared to speak
> for the camera – how naturally they speak – without affectation,
> without posing. I do not think this is a result of naivety or a lack
> of sophistication. Many of their ideas were anything but naïve.
> I think many have a natural courage, frankness and sincerity.
> (Nemtin and Low, 1972: 1)

Because this was 1967 and the widespread use of portable video was not yet a reality, film was sent back to film board headquarters in Montreal for processing and editing. The films were edited vertically and presented in linear sequences, each personality allowed to reflect his or her views.

> When I went to Fogo Island I thought that I would make one, or
> perhaps two or three films. But as the project developed, I found
> that people were much freer when I made short vertical films:
> each one the record of a single interview, or a single occasion. In
> the end I did not do any inter-cutting at all, because if you inter-
> cut people on the basis of issues, what usually happens is that
> you get one person who is all wrong, one person who is partly
> right, and a third person who is right. He becomes the smart guy,
> who puts the others down. This putting down can harm people
> within a community. (Nemtin and Low, 1972: 4)

Through the personalities island issues did emerge: the inability to organize; the need for communication; the common resentment at the idea of resettlement and the sense that government was making decisions about their future from far away without any consultation with the community.

Not sure what to do next with the material, the president of Memorial University and key staff flew to the film board offices in Montreal to discuss the next steps. The president (Lord Taylor) felt the films were too inflammatory to be shown to anyone. The staff didn't agree. There was, says a fellow staff member, a general revolt and many threatened to resign. At dinner that evening, a journalist who had just written a book on Joey Smallwood suggested to his dejected companions that they show the films to the premier and his cabinet.

The screening for the premier and his cabinet did take place in 1968 at Memorial University. At first it was thought that people from Fogo should attend the screening but this proposal was turned down – wisely, for it allowed the politicians to view the films without an antagonistic audience sitting in on the process. Those who attended the session reported that the impact of the films was profound. A film board official described the experience:

> Finally we had fishermen talking to Cabinet ministers. If you take fishermen to the Cabinet, they don't talk about the problems of their lives the way they will among other fishermen. But if you let government people look at the films of fishermen talking together, the message comes through. (Gwyn, 1972: 5)

The message did come through. The minister of fisheries, Aiden Maloney was asked to respond to some of the comments and present the government point of view. Memorial University arranged to interview Maloney and that tape was subsequently shown back to the islanders. That was the first back-and-forth use of the material between communities and decision-makers – another part of the Fogo Process was born.

It is important to realize that the process was allowed to evolve through happenstance. In those days people (well, perhaps not the president) were not so afraid of failure. It was, says Paul MacLeod, a close colleague of Snowden, a different time and it worked a whole lot better. It allowed both for innovation and for failure. We hadn't yet got ourselves into the 'industrialization' of development.

At the beginning, for example, it was not defined that people would have editing rights to their material. The actual screening of the films back to communities came in later experiments in Port aux

Choix and the Labrador coast. In 1968 and 1969 the idea of 'playback' began to take shape and subsequently became a critical component of the process: giving the individual the opportunity to screen and edit the films.

At first people found it difficult to discuss contentious issues in public. The extension team had to get used to long silences after a screening. But discussion did come later, in many cases over a drink at the bar or in someone's house. Through the films, the people began to see that each community across the island was experiencing similar problems. Indeed, it was through the viewing of each other and themselves that an awareness of the problems emerged. The lack of organization was realized. Mistakes were recognized. The Fogo Island Community saw itself more objectively then ever before. Later the parish priest from Port aux Choix, Father Desmond McGrath, commenting on an extension of the Fogo Process in that community, observed, 'I would say that the film did this. That it has done the work which the politicians should have been doing for the last twenty or one hundred years.'

So, you are wondering, what in the end happened on Fogo? Well, probably the most important point is that the Fogo islanders did remain on the island. Yes, Joey Smallwood was moved to change his mind. Snowden talked to Wendy about it in 1983.

> Today few people on Fogo speak about the filming, yet many
> believe their lives were changed enormously by it. This can
> never be accurately measured. But it is certain that the fishermen
> formed an island-wide producer's cooperative which handled and
> processed large catches, enabling them to keep the profits on their
> island. Unemployment of able-bodied men disappeared, and gov-
> ernment directed their efforts into helping people to stay... Films
> did not do these things: people did them. There is little doubt,
> however, that film created a sense of awareness and self-confidence
> that was needed for people advocated development to occur.

In a recent interview on the CBC morning show *Sounds Like Canada*, the host, Shelagh Rogers, was interviewing Zita Cobb, a woman who was said to be one of the wealthiest in the country. She had been one of the lucky ones in the IT business. She also happened to be from Fogo Island and had recently left her urban condominium in Ottawa to return to the island to help the community. Her father had been one of the fishermen who suffered from the loss of the cod fishery during Don's time. Now here she was focusing on the development of the tourist industry and her goal to bring high-speed Internet to the island. Like Don she understood that a strong communication infrastructure can be the backbone of development.

Wendy worked with Don for a brief period in Bangladesh. She picks up the story.

Don Snowden: champion

Back in 1982 I was leaving India to work in Bangladesh with CIDA. I was going to work in the grey zone. My job was to introduce the thinking behind communication for development to the Bangladesh programme. My first thought was to search for the most dynamic and best-known champion of communication to work along with me. Don was a Canadian communication champion writ large. When I met him he had just retired as head of the Extension Department for Memorial University in Newfoundland. He did not consider himself to be a communication specialist. He was first and foremost a community development activist who came to believe that if people are given the right tools and shown how to use them they can help themselves better than anyone else can.

Fogo taught Don and his extension staff the power of film and video for community development and it was this that we wanted to introduce to Bangladesh. But before he would allow this, he established some ground rules. I paraphrase his words:

> You have to find an institutional base, an organization, NGO or extension service that has worked for some time with the communities and gained their trust. The organization must be prepared to stay around for an indefinite period to see that things stirred up by the video are carried through. No matter what, never use the video for your own ends and never show the video to others without the permission of those on the film. Don't go into villages and raise expectations that you can't meet. Examine your own motive for any form of intervention and try to consider the far reaching and often unintended consequences.

I can hear Don's voice as he would say these things over and over again. I can see him and watch his laboured breathing when he suffered an asthma attack in conversation with the young Canadian High Commissioner who was critical of the venture. 'I can never understand', Don complained, 'why people think it is perfectly alright to put a lot of money into something concrete like a road or a railway but then kick up a fuss when smaller money is set aside for something as important as information.'

When we got back to Canada I decided to get Don's ideas on tape. I knew that I was hearing something important and wanted to capture his voice and ideas in an effort to really understand the process. A few months later I travelled to his house in St John's, Newfoundland and spent two long sessions taping his memory of Fogo. My purpose was to understand Fogo through the Snowden vision. The idea proved to be prescient.

Don died in India in 1984. He was in Hyderabad attending the first meeting of the National Council for Development Communications; an organization started by his friend Dr Dubey, whom he had met while adapting the Fogo Process to a project with the National Dairy Research Institute in Haryana. He was also in the middle of preparing two papers for the upcoming conference for the Dag Hammarskjöld Foundation's workshops on Methods and Media for Community Development. It was Don's idea to hold this one in Labrador. The Labrador workshop went ahead in Don's memory.

Over thirty years later in Afghanistan, Don's voice came loudly back to me when I worked with Paul MacLeod trying to bring the ideas of Fogo to Afghan NGOs, and very loudly indeed with a young colleague who tried later to adapt these ideas to another short-lived initiative in Kabul 2007.

> The connecting thread through all of Snowden's work was his passionate belief that when people can communicate their thoughts to one another, the possibilities for a better world are virtually unlimited. (Iglauer, 1984b: 8)

Don was, in his biographer's words, a loud, laughing man who loved food, drink, his family and friends. He loved the Inuit of the Canadian Artic, the fishermen of Newfoundland and just about anyone else so long as they weren't bureaucratic. He was passionate about his life, his work, and was able to express this passion through voice and the written word.

In humanity, he wrote, there is so much that is latent, so little
ability to loosen the fear of ourselves, and so much vitality and
sunshine when we do. It may be that some men in some places
may find they walk with more certainty because we have met, and
they have exposed me to their dignity and their unspoken long-
ings which are the same as mine. (Iglauer, 1984a: 7)

Gaston Roberge: champion

Snowden and his staff used film as a catalyst for community development. Gaston Roberge worked with still photography to help slum-
dwellers learn to see themselves in a positive and humane light
(and even perhaps enable them to tap into that latent capability that
Snowden referred in the paragraph above).

Wendy went to visit Father Roberge in Kolkata in the winter of
2008. She stayed at a hotel close to St Xavier's College where Father
Roberge, recently retired from regular teaching of communication,
is still a member of the faculty. In the following account Wendy
describes her meeting with Roberge in his extremely modest room
on the top of the building.

There are potted plants and birdcages lined up on the outside
walkway in front of the Priest quarters on the top floor of St Xavier
College in Kolkata. We get to it via an ancient elevator. Roberge's
desk, where he sits behind piles of books (his own and others), and
his computer are curtained off from his sleeping quarters. At the
time of the interview, he was deeply involved in putting together
a self-teaching book in a format that allows people to dip into it at
any place that is of interest as they now do on the Web. The book
is being published under the title *Media Dancer, Who Sets the Tune?*
The other day he had a look at his most famous book (*Mediation
– The Action of the Media in Our Society*) and realized it is what he
has been dealing with in his writing for the past thirty years.

In the late 1960s Father Gaston Roberge set up a media centre
known as Chitrabani. A young Jesuit priest from Quebec, he had
just returned to Kolkata from the University of California where
he had been sent by his Jesuit superiors to obtain his Master's in
Theatre Arts (Film). Like Snowden, Roberge was a firm believer

in the power of film and television in people's lives. He wanted to provide enlightened access to media for the marginalized communities living in the slums of Kolkata.

At first he thought that Chitrabani (meaning 'picture'/'voice' in Bengali) would begin by giving cameras to slum kids to shoot their own pictures. He soon changed his mind about this. While he found it exciting to see how kids make their own images, he felt that it would not be sustainable. He knew that photography had its own language. He felt it would be better to give some training to fledgling photographers from the area to help them learn to create an image that would portray life in the slums. Chitrabani soon formed a permanent team of skilled photographers who worked with the communities. He taught them to follow the Cartier-Bresson mantra – not to use a telephoto lens so as to force the photographer to get closer to the subject and never to steal an image. For, the photographer does not take but makes images.

In the beginning the people did not want their pictures taken. They did not want further negative portrayal of their lives (as in the iconic photos of men sleeping during the day along the roadways, women using filthy water from the ditches, beggars searching for scraps).

As so often happens, things changed by happenstance. One day, a young Chitrabani photographer went to the area and captured pictures of slum children doing positive things (playing with wire, trying to read, splashing water). He rushed the film to Chitrabani and developed it on the spot. He managed to get the photos back to the area the same day, hanging them in the local dispensary. The impact, said Roberge, was fantastic. The pictures were beautiful. It was the first time in many onlookers' lives that they were able to see themselves in a positive way. After that everyone wanted their picture taken.

A year later, Chitrabani held its own exhibition (a year before the Year of the Child, he pointed out). The photographs created the reaction that he had hoped for. People were astounded at the beauty of life caught in the photos. Roberge laughs at the memory of hearing one well-heeled woman scanning the photos exclaim 'They are just like us!' Could you hope, asked Roberge, for anything better?

The continued support of the Jesuits and the Cardinal Leger Foundation of Montreal allowed Chitrabani to function from the early 1970s. It is still going today, but Father Roberge is no longer involved. He felt that a twenty-five-year lifespan would be more than sufficient. Now, he says, he can't agree with institutions doing the same thing for thirty years (the world changes and they don't, he implies). Already in 1993, he insisted on closing the photograph section. The world, he said, was becoming digitalized and there was no 'dissolve' between analog and digital photography, and since the centre was unable to jump on the digital bandwagon, it was better to stop.

I went to Chitrabani with Father Roberge and looked through drawer after drawer of carefully catalogued black-and-white and colour photos of Calcutta since the 1970s. Over 15,000 photos. There they were, fantastic photos, lying there – history in a box. It reminded me of an earlier visit to India in 2006. I had gone to the Self Employed Women's Association (SEWA) in Ahmedabad to arrange an exchange for Afghan colleagues to witness NGOs using video for community development. SEWA had a long history of activist video and I hoped that my Afghan friends would learn from this visit. The current head of the organization talked about the mile after mile of wonderful tapes used by activist women through-out the decades. They didn't know what to do with them. No one knew what to do with the Chitrabani material either. Roberge was quite concerned by this. But in his eyes, the photographs had served their purpose and, beautiful as they are, he did not mind letting the orchids fade.

Now we know that the idea of giving cameras to people to record their particular experiences is something that is commonplace. I read that Stephen Spielberg was experimenting with giving video cameras to Palestinian and Israeli teenagers and encouraging them to record and exchange their experiences. I haven't asked him myself but I imagine Spielberg was hoping that sharing life experiences as teenagers would enhance the possibility of a later rapprochement. A colleague did the same thing in Afghanistan when she worked teaching women the art of using the camera to record their daily experiences. She tells me her project expected the photographs to 'sensitize' others to Afghan women's daily existence.

Maybe, she said, exposing others to these lives might affect political decisions.

Roberge's views were somewhat similar. Since photography is an art, and expensive at that, he wanted to give slum people not cameras but photographers. He wanted to help people *see* others as they really are. He was struggling with Camus's famous saying about giving a voice to the voiceless. It was, he felt, not really true. In his view, people did have a voice, but what they needed was someone to *hear that voice*. Since it is much more demanding actually to listen, he wanted to find a medium that would catch people's attention and help them *hear* and *understand*.

Development, for Roberge, is anything that can bring us back to being more human. He sees us moving into a post-human society (creation of artificial intelligence etc.) and believes that only those who are more human can bring about actual development. 'If I deal with a person in a humane manner it is the humane manner that matters more than the money – people who live in poverty need money but above all they need a humane gesture – no one can steal it from them once they have received it.' People, he said, often accused Mother Theresa of being impractical. 'But no', he pointed out, 'she was very practical. People were hungry, she gave them food. They needed shelter and she gave them shelter. They were dying and she said "I will stay with you so you won't die alone."' This, he said, is what he means by making you more human.

Governments, he believes, are quite different. Their aim is trying to figure out how to make people do, as they imply, 'what we know they should do'. In his view, even the new effort on the part of the Indian government for community radio is based on reaching out to people to tell them what to do. Roberge and Easterly seem to agree on the dichotomy between listener-searchers and planner-tellers.

In its time Chitrabani created a particular niche. It was the first place in Kolkata where it was possible to learn about film and photography and so it managed to attract a large following of film buffs and communicators. Film as a medium for social change was a strongly popular notion in the 1970s and those in Kolkata who embraced that idea were strong supporters of Chitrabani. 'Kolkata "owned" Chitrabani', observed a colleague. Father Roberge, himself a very modest man, became a well-known figure as its founder.

Roberge and Snowden pioneered their work around the same time, with parallel convictions. Both were champions that had thorough knowledge of their contexts. Both used media as a means to give people dignity and confidence to take control over their destiny. Both illustrate core principles that became part of Another Development a decade later. Ricardo picks up the thread.

Alex Sim: champion

A couple of years ago I was teaching a graduate course in Extension Education at the University of Guelph. I would invite Mark Waldron (by then retired from our programme at Guelph) to speak to the class about his experience with the National Farm Radio Forum (NFRF). I could not think of a better teaching moment than putting students in touch with someone who had lived through one of the most inspiring communication experiments in the country. His use of media was basic: an old cassette player and a long worn-out scroll of Manila paper. He would play us excerpts from the programmes while he unrolled the history of the NFRF on that worn-out scroll. It felt like revisiting history – so special that we videotaped the presentation for posterity.

Mark would begin by explaining that when he was three years old, growing up on a farm in the eastern townships of Quebec, Alex Sim came to visit. Sim was starting the Forum: an experience that would bring news and discussions to farm kitchens across the nation between 1942 and 1965 – predating the work of Snowden and Roberge.

The NFRF was a joint effort by the Canadian Broadcast Corporation (CBC) and the Canadian Association for Adult Education. The NFRF consisted of weekly radio broadcasts combined with listening groups that would send feedback to the broadcasters. The listening groups would discuss the radio programme and prepare a summary of their reactions. Each group would send this summary back to a regional coordinator. This created a two-way communication – every week. The legacy of this process was powerful enough to be exported by UNESCO to India and Ghana.

By reporting the conclusions arrived at in groups in the next broadcast, the members were given a collective voice, a release from the passivity of just listening and discussing. One commentator called this a true social intervention. (Sim, 1998: 3)

The champion in this case was Alex Sim. I met him in Guelph weeks before he died. He was full of stories, his memory crisp while his eyes and ears were failing. After every idea, he would reach out and give me a copy of something he had written. I left his house with a pile of typewritten reports and monographs. I also left with the feeling that I had met a champion, someone with an unwavering commitment to what we have come to realize is best expressed though the principles of Another Development.

Alex was one of the champions that made NFRF one of the largest adult education programmes in the country. In 1950–51, 1,606 listener groups were registered with 20,769 participants. At the time, for rural Canada, these numbers were very significant. 'A joke current among NFRF leaders was the claim that the program had a large audience in Ottawa made up of politicians and civil servants who used the occasion to put their ears to the ground' (Sim, 1998: 3).

The NFRF slogan was 'Read Listen Discuss Act – which represented an underlying assumption that people could do something about the problems that beset them. Some issues lent themselves to local solutions, but others called for governmental action. In either case, education should precede action' (Sim, 1998: 3). Alex explained how NFRF lost political support after the war – the orchid's days were counted; how a fear of socialism contributed to its demise as the Cold War began.

One amusing episode illustrates the temper of the times, the relentless scrutiny to which the program was subjected and the populist nonchalance of those who were fashioning the experiment. A translation of a Danish folk song was popular in some farm groups. It was decided the theme music would be a male quartet singing its first verse:

Men of the soil we have laboured unending
We have fed the world with the grain we have sown
Now with the dawn of a new day ascending
Giants of the earth at last we rise to claim our own.

Needless to say the critics grumbled about its musicality as well as what they claimed its incendiary message. Finally after several years of grumbling a typical Canadian compromise was arrived at. The quartet was retained but only allowed to hum the music. Of course most of the farm people across the country already knew the words. (Sim, 1998: 6)

I can still hear the song – it was one of the ones that Mark played for us on the cassettes.

Looking back sixty-five years later, Sim was pleased that the experiment had left a legacy. What is clear is that the Farm Radio Forum existed thanks to champions like Alex Sim who knew the context of their time and had a commitment to the rural people. Like so many of our orchids, it passed away, but it left its mark. Enough Canadians eh! Here is a taste of a champion from the South.

Manuel Calvelo-Rios: champion

When I first started to work at FAO in Rome I kept on hearing about the achievements of project managers in the field. They took on an Indiana Jones image for me: getting things done out there, far away from the office, notwithstanding the constant nagging of the bureaucracy. People like Manuel Calvelo-Rios, Santiago Funes, Hector Wong, Alberto Troilo and Luis Masias had all managed to do innovative work with rural communities. Many of them at some point or another had worked with Manuel. He has set the tone for FAO's work in Latin America. It was an orchid all right, and its name was *pedagogía audiovisual* (audiovisual pedagogy), and, like the Farm Radio Forum and the Fogo Process, efforts had been made to transplant this orchid to other continents.

Pedagogía audiovisual or audiovisual pedagogy was started in Peru in the early 1970s. It focused on video-based training for farmers. The champion behind it was Manuel Calvelo-Rios. At the time, Manuel was very critical of the conventional extension system. He disliked the standard, unidirectional flow of information from 'expert' to farmer that prevailed in agricultural extension. He realized that farmers knew a lot. As he developed training materials using video and supporting guidebooks, he began by recording what they knew. The approach started by documenting vanishing indigenous agricultural technology on video and making it available to other farmers. The information was provided in such a way that farmers would actually learn from the modules. Manuel was fundamentally a teacher and a good one. In Argentina he had pioneered the use of television to enable university courses to reach more students. This method was about teaching and learning. It reached large numbers of farmers through repeated small-group sessions organized by trained facilitators. Since the technology was not yet portable, Manuel and his team designed boxes so that even mules could carry the playback equipment to the field to be powered with car batteries. I found their zest inspiring.

Like Fogo, *pedagogía audiovisual* emerged in a context that has strong historical roots. The government of General Velazco launched a national agrarian reform programme in 1969. As part of the programme, a national training centre was created, the Centro Nacional de Capacitación e Investigación para la Reforma Agraria, (CENCIRA). This was also the time when the Canadian government launched its Challenge for Change programme. In a case study on this Peruvian experience, our colleague Colin Fraser made the connection with the Fogo Process. He explained how an approach like Fogo could only thrive under the right political environment. The same was true for CENCIRA: it was part of a progressive effort at land reform that enjoyed support from Allende's government in Chile. Starting in 1974 FAO and UNDP supported CENCIRA and created the conditions for *pedagogía audiovisual* to thrive (Fraser, 1987; Santiago Funes, personal communication).

Audiovisual pedagogy took information right into the farm and in a language that was understandable. The training modules were combined with hands-on exercises. During an evaluation 90 per cent of farmers confirmed that the videos were 'very understandable'. They said that watching them was much like being out in the field. Manuel worked on the approach with relentless enthusiasm. By the time I met him, he had polished it into a strict training methodology. Trainees of the approach had to survive a gruelling 32-day training programme with no breaks. They came out knowing every angle to the approach. These were not documentaries, they were modules for learning, each crafted with minute attention.

At the time the approach was seen as a challenge by conventional extension programmes. Instead of specialists instructing farmers, it was about farmers teaching farmers on video. The national extension system of Peru ended up rejecting the approach. The organizational culture could not handle it. Calvelo-Rios and FAO then took the approach to many other countries, and from that work a solid cadre of communication specialists emerged. They are still at it, growing their own orchids when the conditions are right.

Back then I was a bureaucrat never able to take thirty-two days off my busy routine at the office, so I never took the endurance test of a *pedagogía audiovisual* course – I wish I had. On the other hand I did travel with Manuel through Latin America developing a regional project. We used to get into all kinds of debates, intense ones. To cool things down he would always close by saying: 'I only fight with my friends.'

We met these early champions and they have left us with a sense of awe. They all decided to get things done no matter what (immediate action is necessary and possible). They did not have an ounce of naivety: they were very political in their outlook and knew that they were only able to shift things a little (Another Development requires structural transformation). Some had survived political strife in more than one place, only to transplant their lives and start anew in another. They understood the big picture, they understood the development industry, and they acted notwithstanding its straitjacket. Most important, they stayed in place for a long time and got to know the context well. This allowed them to zero in on what mattered most to rural and marginal communities (geared to the satisfaction of needs, beginning with the eradication of poverty). The Latin Americans, just like the Canadians, had a sincere commitment to enabling people's innate capacity to improve their own predicament (endogenous and self-reliant, that is, relying on the strength of the societies which undertake it).

Our stories and the core principles of Another Development come together and set the scene for our argument. Those champions found ways to use methods and media that were unprecedented. We now study what they did and see how they combined advocacy, educational and participatory communication functions. At the time they did not have this fancy classification; they simply followed their gut feeling. Those guts, though, were full of principles that have managed to travel into the present.

SEVEN

New activists:
principles that travel

In the last chapter we told stories about people who had pioneered new ways of working with established media. Most of the stories illustrated applications of participatory communication functions (helping people express their needs); advocacy communication (getting voices heard by others so that change might happen) and educational communication (helping farmers learn from each other). You will have noticed that all of them were men; Wendy continues.

A sign of the times, I have to tell you. Last year I went with a friend to a CIDA retirement lunch. She and I had worked together on the CIDA Bangladesh programme in 1982. When we walked into the room, I was taken aback to see (what seemed to me) only a roomful of white-haired men. I turned to my friend with an unspoken question. You forget, she said, that back then there were hardly any women at CIDA. Fortunately times have changed: in the NGO where I now work there are mostly women. We need balance.

In this chapter we share stories about today's activists. They are champions who also embrace Another Development. The principles have travelled and these activists are putting them to work in today's context. They have found ways of working outside the grey zone and they are using current media in innovative ways.

There is nothing new, writes Leonard Henny (1983), about using moving images in social processes. He describes how two pioneer Soviet film-makers, right after the revolution in the early 1920s, organized a film train equipped with cameras and film projection facilities to go on tour through Russian villages to show films about new ways of life in post-revolutionary Russia. The two film-makers stopped in villages to show films on alcoholism and tuberculosis. They also made films on the spot, processing them in the lab aboard the train, to play back immediately to the people for discussion.

The coming of Stalinism brought an early end to the project, but not before their work could become an inspiration to media collectives founded in Europe and Japan in the latter part of the 1960s. What the film-makers had been putting into reality was the theoretical work of Sergei Tretyakov, who argued that a new society needs a new relationship between the author/artist and the public and that the artist's job is to make people write their own history and stage their own drama (Henny, 1983).

This sounds very like Father Roberge, who continues to argue for a new relationship between the filmmaker and society. When Wendy asked him if he had ever thought of any follow up to his work with Chitrabani (helping people see themselves in a positive light and helping others see a certain reality), he replied: 'More often than not, the products are not really used. Too much stress is placed on the media person when the real stress should be on the activist.' She asked him if he felt that all development workers should be activists. 'I invite them to do so', he said – 'otherwise development can be a good job with good money.'

Stalin K., who with a group of like-minded activists founded the Indian NGO Drishti, said almost exactly the same thing: 'Professionals are people who work in development for the sake of the job and the money it brings whereas activists are there for social change and stay with the process.'

Drishti: activist video champions

Stalin K. is definitely an activist. This Stalin was born in Kerala to ardent Marxists. After earning his Master's in Communication and Media Studies (and spending all his money on a video camera), he migrated to Ahmedabad in 1991 where he co-founded the Drishti Media Collective. Drishti, says their website, is a 'leading human rights and development organization that uses media, communication and the arts to strengthen India's social movements and organizations, in order to extend their reach and to increase the participation of marginalized communities'.

It was SEWA that indirectly introduced Stalin to the power of video. SEWA is the Self-Employed Women's Association, known for its early work with video advocacy work. The director of SEWA had met video pioneer Martha Stuart in the 1980s at a workshop in Mali. She invited Martha to Ahmedabad to help train SEWA members (street vendors, vegetable sellers, garment workers) to use video to portray the difficulties of their lives. These films were used both to confront bureaucracy (films showed police harassment of small-scale vendors) and to provide a powerful vehicle for horizontal exchanges of experience between self-employed women all over the country.

Drishti took this notion and worked with it to train NGOs to use video for their own work. Later they began to train community people directly to manage their own media. As they like to say: 'you are training an NGO film-maker who might move; the village person will not move.'

This has not been easy. As ever, funding presents a major obstacle since most donors are willing to finance a 'one-off' film but do not even comprehend the need for an ongoing process. Drishti people commented that they even have difficulties convincing their NGO partners and the communities that the learning is not about making one film but about learning a skill. Their course extends over an eighteen-month period. Wendy takes it from here.

I have visited Drishti (meaning 'vision') twice over the past few years and been entirely captivated by the zeal with which they are engaged in their work. The small Drishti team and I talked at length about the excitement they feel for their profession. 'Now', they explained, 'our work has evolved because of the reaction of the communities. When we were only filmmakers our work stopped at the making of the film. Now, we find that this is where our work really begins ... the screening of the film becomes the high point – this is where we all talk and talk and talk with people about taking action.'

Professional media makers' work is done when they file the story or when they hand over the finished edited tape. In contrast, the work is barely beginning for the participatory video makers. He or she will be involved in facilitating playbacks of the tape, in building on the insight, motivation and understanding the tape creates, and in continuing working toward the long-term goals that the tape is serving. (Stuart, 1989)

Luckily we got a chance to drop in to one of the video centres in the poor area of the city after my meeting with Drishti. Drishti had been able to team up with the NGO Saath, which worked in the area; it was Saath that had been able to rise the funding for the venture (with the Drishti video component buried within). Saath is focused on making slum areas in Ahmedabad a more equitable living environment.

The women and men who greeted us were very friendly but matter-of-fact. One woman ended up doing most of the talking and a friend translated. She explained how she had been working with Saath in her community for some time but had always relied on interpersonal communication, but it was difficult to take this to scale (her words). The filming, she said, has allowed them to reach out to many more areas, it has created a social network.

She told the story of one film they had produced on the subject of ration shops. It centred on the corruption of these shops – the siphoning off of food and the black market in kerosene and oil. 'We all knew the problems', she said, 'but there was nothing we could do about them.'

There was a call box set up where people could call and make complaints and occasionally someone's complaints would be answered – the community producer made a point of not leaving this fact out and included the call box in the film. At the same time they filmed the problems women face getting into the shop. They showed graphically the way that kerosene was siphoned off and interviewed the government ration officer and recorded the government response.

They screened this film in all the communities: they went from slum to slum and set up little outdoor theatres in the laneways between the houses; they would hang up the screen and plug the projector into someone's house nearby. After the screening there would be a great deal of discussion – Does this film relate to your reality? Is there anything here to help you cope with this problem?

These screenings led to a flood of complaints bombarding city hall. There were raids on the ration shops. People found the courage to tell the shopkeepers to stop cheating them. They also went to the Food Control Office and did a screening there, forcing the food controller to do something about the situation. Most importantly they showed the film to the Ration Shopkeepers' Association and managed to get all the stakeholders together to discuss the film and its findings.

The film has had a major impact and the cheating has stopped. The Ration Shopkeepers' Association has come to the video office and told the community producers of their own problems and has asked the team to film their story. The team is still negotiating. When asked about the process and the learning, the women replied: 'We are still in kindergarten but there are so many issues, and we will not stop until they are all covered. There is not a single issue we will not tackle – we are not afraid of anyone!'

I asked them if they thought that people would get tired of watching films. There is no end, they said, to the possible stories: 'We are not making movies about Saath but we are telling people's stories. Every day at least two dozen issues come up. We have five locations and every month we reach about 7,000 people.'

We asked to see short clips of the films. They were terrific and gripping. The ration story film was particularly brilliant: the village producers acted like *60 Minutes* producers and told the story interwoven with the scenes and the individual interviews.

What captured our attention with Drishti and Saath is the commitment to the principles of Another Development by these activist champions. They know their context; they made a deliberate effort to work with the advocacy, participatory and educational functions of communication. We celebrate their willingness to work outside the confines of a development industry that cannot fit their achievements into its plans and fund their work. These activists refuse to work in the grey zone. They stay with the picture. We now shift to West Africa, where Alex and Wilna Quarmyne have championed community radio.

Alex and Wilna Quarmyne:
activist community radio champions

In the last chapter we mentioned that UNESCO had experimented with the Canadian Farm Forum format in Ghana and India. This was in 1964. In India this became known as the Pune experiment after the town selected for the site. In Ghana they selected Ada, a fishing village on the east coast. The experiment flared and died. Thirty years later, Ada was the chosen site for the community radio station, Radio Ada, started by community radio enthusiasts Alex and Wilna Quarmyne.

Radio Ada became the catalyst for the formation of the Ghana Community Radio Network (GCRN), the association of community radio stations and initiatives in Ghana. Alex and Wilna Quarmyne are co-founders and continue to be volunteers of both the radio and the network. Wendy found this statement by Wilna which sums up their basic motivation: 'GCRN regards the airwaves like seas and rivers, as a basic natural resource. Like all natural resources, rights and equitable allocation are central issues. GCRN considers that marginalized communities have a prior right to use the airwaves for their own development' (White, 2007).

Alex Quarmyne's broadcasting career began in Liberia in the early 1950s and included several years as a producer with the Los Angeles community radio station KPFK. In the 1960s he had been sent by UNESCO from Ghana to help set up the broadcasting department of the Institute of Mass Communication at the University of the Philippines. One of Alex's students did his Master's thesis on one of the first community radio stations in the Philippines, DZJO. Around that time Wilna opted out of a broadcasting career in Manila to live in the then isolated rural town of Infanta, Quezon, to help set up the station. This is where she met Alex. DZJO was launched in 1967 and is still going strong today. Wilna mentioned that when Quezon province had a terrible mudslide in 2004 the radio station was buried along with much of Infanta and the surrounding towns served by the community radio station. That could have been its end, but a survey was run with the survivors to ask what they felt were the priorities for restoration. The revival of the community radio station was the number one priority.

It was inevitable that getting community radio started in Africa would be part of Alex and Wilna's agenda. Until the 1990s broadcasting in the continent was operated almost exclusively as a state monopoly. In the 1970s, while a military regime was still in power, they applied for a frequency to set up a community radio station in Ghana. The application was turned down. In the early 1980s Alex, who was then based in Nairobi as UNESCO Regional Communication Adviser for Africa, was instrumental in the establishment of the Homa Bay Community Radio Station. It was shut down in the wake of the 1982 coup attempt in Kenya. In Zimbabwe, Wilna worked closely with the Federation of African Media Women on the Development through Radio (DTR) project and organized with them a workshop in 1990 to introduce the idea of starting a community radio station. The rural women who ran the DTR listening clubs turned the idea down because they felt the government would never allow them to operate an independent radio station.

On their return to Ghana in January 1995 Alex and Wilna tried again. Three years earlier, the new constitution had restored democratic civilian rule. Soon after their return the government called for applications for radio frequency authorizations. The couple managed to put in the first application for a community radio station by the mid-March deadline. In May 1996, after a lot of legwork, they were issued the authorization to operate a community radio station in Ada.

Ada, Alex's hometown, was the logical place to start. Alex had been away for nearly thirty years, but they gathered enough from their initial enquiries to know that too many people had made promises that they could not deliver. They didn't want to add themselves to that list. They decided not to tell the larger community about their intentions until they actually got the broadcast authorization. However, to ensure that the project would not be seen as underhand, they took into their confidence two key must-know people in Ada, a leading traditional authority (chief) and the head of the local government administration. When they finally got the frequency they arranged for local town criers to beat the gong gong (traditional bell) to call for volunteers. Wilna told what happened then.

> The volunteers enthusiastically undertook a participatory research activity to ask the community first what they thought of the

idea of their own community radio station and, if the response was positive, to listen closely to what they wanted it to be like. To listen especially to the voices of those who are normally not heard.

The community asked for a radio station that has a strong cultural base; is rooted in their experience; is broadcast in the local language; gives a voice to the voiceless; and promotes unity. Wilna continued:

> Radio Ada has now been on the air for ten years, but the outcome of that first participatory research continues to guide its spirit and its direction: to live out its slogan – to be 'the voice of the Dangme people', especially those traditionally excluded – on a day-to-day basis.

Many of those initial volunteers continue to be mainstays at Radio Ada. They are the original examples of the station's thinking that, as Wilna puts it, 'every community member is a potential radio producer'. Alex and Wilna made a deliberate decision not to use 'professional' broadcasters because, they said, they 'are trained to talk, not listen'. Working together, they trained the first batch of producers, news reporters and announcers, who put the station on the air. The training necessarily covered the technical aspects. Most important, though, was bringing out their ability to engage with the community because, Alex said, 'the person holding the mike and the recorder are only facilitators for the real producers: the community members.'

For the first three months after the station went on the air the Quarmynes worked alongside the volunteers night and day. Then they gradually withdrew to let the volunteers take over the complete running and management of the station. Many of these volunteers have themselves become champions of community radio.

Each year the Quarmynes are part of Radio Ada's strategic and evaluation sessions; built-in evaluation is a hallmark of the station. When asked for an example of the strength of the community radio process, Wilna related a story she says she likes to tell often because it shows what community radio is really about. At one evaluation she asked the facilitator to raise a hypothetical question: 'What would you do if Radio Ada were to be taken away?' People were shocked at the question and started shouting at the idea – 'You can't take it away!' When they had calmed down, one woman explained: 'If you take Radio Ada away from us, we will lose our language and lose our culture. We will lose who we are.'

We could go on and tell you more about how, anchored in Radio Ada and working with GCRN, the Quarmynes are helping to lay the foundations for at least one hundred community radio stations in Ghana. Suffice to say their work is rooted in a commitment to Another Development. Like Drishti they live by those principles; that is what keeps them going. The same convictions drive our next champion, this one on the other side of Africa.

Minou Fuglesang: an activist champion who does not mince words

We met Minou quite by happenstance. She was sitting next to us in a workshop at a communication conference. We were startled when we heard her name and leaned forward to ask her if she was indeed Andreas Fuglesang's daughter. An anthropologist by training, she says that her father's ideas were embedded in her very being. Andreas sought to see the world as others see it: visual literacy. For Minou this translated into her present role of heading an organization, Femina HIP in Tanzania, producing print and audiovisual material on sexual health that resonates with youth and communities across the country. In the past, Tanzanian society shunned open, public discussion on such sensitive issues but, with the HIV epidemic, things have changed.

Canada's *Globe and Mail* published an article (23 August 2008) about today's teenage girls having less sex and being more sexually responsible. The girls said this was the direct result of the comprehensive sex education they received at school. When Dr Minou Fuglesang went to Tanzania from Sweden in the 1990s, she found that quite the opposite was true. Rather, lack of knowledge and discussion on essential life skills issues such as sexuality and HIV prevention was the norm. With a team of young Tanzanians she set out to change this situation. She founded and coordinated a multimedia health information initiative. In the past, she explained, traditional initiation rites guided communication on sexuality and responsible behaviour for young people in the tribal contexts. These have gradually disappeared or lost their significant function, as in many other African countries (Fuglesang, 1997). Sadly, the modern school system has not been able to assume the role of transmitter of life skills concerning sexuality issues. Implementation of sexuality and HIV/AIDS information in schools curricula has been slow, and met with reluctance on moral grounds; many have feared that this type of education will encourage promiscuity.

In 1999 Fuglesang launched Femina HIP, a civil society 'edutainment' (a combination of education and entertainment) initiative for youth using an existing, glossy magazine as its flagship product. Its magazine *Fema* had began its life as *Femina*, a fashion magazine but soon expanded to cover real-life testimonials, the drama of everyday life, accompanied by useful information on how to reduce risk and protect against pregnancy and sexually transmitted disease. The information was direct and to the point, always using people's own stories and voices as a point of departure. *Fema* would play with the local metaphors but did not shy away from words that are explicit.

Minou took the time to understand how the young in Tanzania interpret content of texts but also visuals like photographs, cartoons, colours, style and patterns. She was fascinated by the realization that people do not necessarily see things in the same way. This insight lies at the core of every activity in the health information initiative that she now directs. She and her team want to be sure they are sensitive to others' perceptions – it is all about cultural sensitivity and about understanding. Feedback and formative research are therefore key to the approach.

Today Femina HIP is known for its frank, open and direct manner of communication in Tanzania and its criticism of the ABC approach long touted as the way to control HIV/AIDS in East Africa (A for Abstinence, B for Being faithful, C for Condoms). Femina HIP has responded to this by promoting what it calls the sexual health alphabet. Minou explains that people need to be fully literate in sexuality. In this alphabet there is a word for every letter – P for penis, K for Kiss, M for Masturbation. 'We need to know these words and use them openly' (personal communication). She insists that when talking about body parts or sexual acts we need to make sure that people understand the meaning of the words and the concepts and do not shy away from talking about any of them. 'People love the alphabet approach', she explains. In the same process Femina HIP tries to push the boundaries of sensitivities not only of individuals but also of the gatekeepers.

> The reason why we have had such a lot of support and little censorship is probably because we let people speak up about their experiences and views about lifestyles and sexuality. It is always their perspective that is the point of departure. We try not to preach and only convey facts. (Gossé, 2006)

Minou Fuglesang has stayed to help the project grow. *Femina* changed its title to *Fema*, female and male, to incorporate its growing audience of both young men and women. Circulation has risen to 160,000 copies, produced four times a year. This is currently the largest print run of any magazine or newspaper in eastern Africa. The Femina HIP multimedia initiative now produces other media products: another magazine, *Si Mchezo!*, targeting semi-literate youth communities in the rural areas; a television talk show; booklets; an interactive, bilingual website on sexual health, and reader clubs and road shows. Each medium complements the others.

> We are rooted in the concept of communication for social change. Our agenda is not only to focus on individuals but to seek wider community mobilization. Furthermore, we understand that individuals are influenced by national discourse so we work at all levels in recognition of this reality. We have been pushing to get sexual education into the school system. This is dependent of course on the national policy environment, the government, as much as it is with the gatekeepers of the school. By 2006 we started to see a shift. A policy for HIV and life-skills education was put in place but there are still few curriculum texts. *Fema* magazine, on the other hand, entered the schools informally, through the back door, as extracurricular material but has by far become the biggest school initiative engaging secondary students and teachers across the country in the sexual health and HIV prevention issues. (personal communication)

Femina HIP's approach reminds us of the importance of understanding the context from the inside. Culture is at the heart of our last example. Culture is also at the heart of the next. We take you back to a different context, northern Canada. Ricardo picks up the thread.

Brian Beaton: activist Internet champion

For some years now I have been invited to collaborate with Keewaytinook Okimakanak (KO), an Aboriginal organization in the remote north-west region of the province of Ontario, Canada. This all started when Brian Beaton came to Guelph in 1998 for a workshop. Brian is the manager of K-Net, the provider of information and communication services and content for the KO communities. He told us how the KO chiefs wanted computers in the schools for the children in the north. K-Net has brought high-speed Internet to communities that only a decade ago had no phones. It is the most advanced Aboriginal-owned and -operated network in the country. As soon as I met Brian I could tell he was a champion, stubborn to the core – nothing seemed to get in the way of his commitment to help the First Nations take control over their future.

K-Net is based in Sioux Lookout, in the boreal forest of northwestern Ontario. You could fit France into this region. But this is an area with a population of approximately 45,000 people (Nishnawbe Aski Nation, n.d.). Many of the communities are only accessible by airplane, except for a few weeks in winter when roads over frozen lakes are open. These communities face harsh conditions, the result of a colonization legacy that has left a generation struggling to define its identity. The context is the Third World of the North.

Before K-Net existed, when KO wanted to send information to the communities, they would drop flyers off small planes. Today they have connectivity as good as in any urban centre: a change in technology that baffles the mind. This has happened in a traditional culture where the elders were recently living off the land. Together with other colleagues I have had the privilege to document this fast-moving train (Ramírez and Richardson, 2005).

When I first visited K-Net in 1999 Brian introduced me to his team: Dan Pellerin, Jesse Fiddler and a few others. They function as a team of champions and most of them are still there. They handle proposal jargon as easily as cables and modems, but they have never lost sight of the community focus. This combination of skills is shared by all of the other champions discussed in this chapter.

They made a start by putting satellite connections into schools and health stations. They applied for every single funding programme available. It did not take long before blue cables ran under the snow – from the nursing station into the homes. People who had been without a phone began using email. Thanks to connectivity, KO has produced an Internet-based high school allowing young people to stay in their communities to finish their education. They have established a telemedicine programme to bring quality care to the remote communities. Their work serves as a role model across Canada.

K-Net is an organization that defends First Nation community development needs. It is run by champions who negotiate with government funding agencies and telecommunication corporations, to make sure they introduce technology and applications that are relevant. They always keep their focus on providing local content. It is a locally built response to an environment of isolation and the high cost of travel. It is there to stay as part of the Aboriginal organization that it belongs to. Its champions have created relationships of trust with stakeholders inside the KO communities and with many in the outside world.

When I look back I realize how both the First Nations culture and K-Net were open to experiment with participatory planning exercises. These methods have a history in international development but they were new to rural and remote Canada. I take you back to a cold winter morning in late November 1999 in Fort Severn, the most northerly community in Ontario, when we tried some of the exercises. While it was many degrees below zero outside, inside the room was warm. It was not just the temperature, I still recall the smell of coffee – the Cree have a way of making you feel at home. The chief told us he would be late, but he had made sure that we were welcomed by a group of youth, of men and women from across the community; people with leadership skills and a sense of community. We asked to share their ideas and hopes for better health, for better education, and for a better economy.

The workshop was about listening before going ahead with the establishment of the high-speed network. People told us why they wanted the technology, and how they would use it. They explained what success would be in their own terms. I paraphrase their answer:

> If you come back in five years and our Internet high school is working, you will hear a whistle. That will be your indicator. You see, if we can keep more of our youth in the community, instead of them moving away for high school, we will have enough of them for some hockey games.

Jesse Fiddler created visual summaries of the workshop and uploaded them to the K-Net website – the images were up within hours, a first for me (K-Net, 1999). The process became visible to the outside world. These images helped make 'community engagement' a popular term inside the offices of Industry Canada in the nation's capital. According to Brian Beaton, this work helped win the 1999 competition to become a national demonstration project. The Kuh-ke-nah Network of SMART First Nations became a case study and it has since attracted interest from Aboriginal organizations around the world.

K-Net has a commitment to working with and for the communities it serves. It discovered long ago that information and communication technology only makes sense when it responds to needs. This fits with Another Development. K-Net is not alone: this basic premiss has been documented the world over (Berger and Neuhaus, 1977; Carlson, 1999; de Jager, 2006; Warren, 2007). For this technology to work, it needs to be driven by a commitment to community development.

A common focus

We have a hunch that if we were to put these champions in one room the following would happen. They would emphasize the very principles that drove the early champions; and they would do it through stories not fancy words. They would not give themselves much credit. They would explain how urgent the work really is; they would worry about how much work needs to be done for structural transformation. Lastly, they would explain how the context established what was possible; and it is to context we return, so obvious and yet so often forgotten.

EIGHT

The forgotten context

We dedicated the last two chapters to champions. We now turn to context to round out our discussion on coordinates. Context is complex because it has many dimensions. It is all encompassing. At the very least context is *community* – with its various interpretations. It is the *organizations* with which we work, ranging from small groups to established *institutions*. It is also the *geography* and *history* of the places where we work. Context is people's *culture, political systems, media* and *funding* rules. These are all interconnected.

We are of the opinion that context matters a great deal and fear that it is something that is often overlooked.

> Environments are not passive wrappings, but are, rather, active processes which are invisible. The ground rules, pervasive structure, and over-all patterns of environments elude easy perception. (McLuhan and Fiore, 1967: 68)

McLuhan and Fiore challenge us to make environments (context) more visible. This is the motivation to write this chapter. We begin with examples from colleagues who have come to realize how much the nature of the organization dictates what can be done. Ricardo has a story to illustrate this point.

Organizations are half the methodology

The farmers' market in Guelph is a place to catch up on gossip and meet friends. A few months ago while I was looking for free-range eggs I bumped into a colleague. She teaches at the university and has years of experience in Honduras, among other places. I had not seen her for ages. She is an accomplished sociologist who specializes in participatory approaches to agriculture. So I started telling her about our book. Something hit a nerve when I mentioned context. She had just been invited to talk about her approach during a national forum on ecology in Mexico. The hosts were so pleased with her presentation on participatory plant breeding that they wanted her back to replicate the approach across the country. However, she was not sure. Something told her the environment was not right. It was the organizations, she realized – they were not the same as the ones in Central America. The context, she suspected would not be able to nurture the approach she had helped establish in Honduras.

Our second example echoes our colleague's experience. It comes from the practitioners of 'Reflect', a participatory literacy methodology. They explain that 'the extent to which methods will be adopted is heavily influenced by the nature of institution or organization that takes it up' (Nandago, 2007: 33). This confirms what we have often said: the nature of the organization is half the methodology. This brings us to those champions whom we know inside large organizations. We admire how they struggle to create a space for participatory communication work, and how often the window closes – we have been there. A major reason that Ricardo was able to experiment with participatory communication while at FAO was that Silvia Balit, the head of the unit, made space for him. She acknowledged this herself and felt that her role was to keep the bureaucracy at bay. Most champions we have mentioned have had a godparent in the system that kept the funds flowing and let them get on with their work. Without this type of support we are all very vulnerable.

Earlier we spoke of our experience in Mozambique struggling with a communication strategy for the new National Water Policy. Wendy has a sequel to that story. We mentioned that the policy had been promoted by the World Bank to present a completely different approach to the provision of drinking water. In keeping with the times, the policy called for 'a demand-driven' approach. This meant that the government had to change from implementer to facilitator and develop a strategy that empowers a community to implement a water supply system that it is willing and able to sustain. Communities had to begin by putting in an application for a new borehole (demand), organize to pay a portion of the cost (user pay), and commit to ongoing operation and maintenance. As is the custom of the World Bank, money was put aside for a 'demonstration' project where the tenets of the new policy were to be tested on the ground. One of the directors of the Department of Rural Water was put in charge of the project. Wendy met him after almost a year into the project. He was downcast and discouraged. He told her that the Bank was not happy with his performance. He was bewildered. He had taken the ideas of the new policy to heart and had gone to great pains to ensure that communities 'were mobilized' prior to drilling the boreholes. This, it turned out, was the problem. At the annual water conference in Washington, Wendy ran into the task manager for the project. She asked the woman just why the Bank was unhappy with the direction of the project. 'Ah', she said, 'sometimes we forget that the Bank is, well, actually a bank. We were unhappy because he had taken a full year without disbursing funds. This to a bank is unacceptable.' The project director returned from Washington and began drilling boreholes. The Bank was pleased with this performance.

We imagine that many can relate to this Mozambican story. Large donors have a tendency to say one thing but actually do another. The organizational ethos and structure really do dictate eventual implementation. This so often gets buried in such strong rhetoric that for one moment we think it (the rhetoric) might be real. We come back again and again to thinking about the word 'intent'. In the end, as the woman said, a bank is a bank.

Remote Aboriginal communities responding to history

The K-Net story in the previous chapter is immersed in an Aboriginal context of geographical isolation combined with a tragic history of colonization. What those communities and their organizations are doing to regain their pride and self-control is in line with most core principles of Another Development. This is possible thanks to partnerships that thrived in the 1990s with funding from provincial and federal programs. Yet those programmes are fragile in this age of shrinking public funding, and today the policy environment is no longer favourable. Ironically, while information and communication technologies (ICTs) have been part and parcel of this era of homogenization, K-Net ran with them to reduce isolation and provide health and education in their own terms.

K-Net as an organization is an expression of Aboriginal culture that is healing from a history of colonization. K-Net is accountable to the chiefs of the five communities of Keewaytinook Okimakanak, and this gives the organization a commitment to the grassroots. It has evolved in a geographic area that is vast and isolating. It is a home-grown organization that could not have been designed from the outside. It has been the vehicle to keep champions in place.

It is clear to us that the context shaped the K-Net way of being and of doing things. You cannot 'upscale' K-Net or 'replicate it', as planners are so tempted to do. While K-Net has been able to expand services to other Aboriginal councils across northern Ontario, it is the principles that travel to other contexts, where local champions may adapt them to suit their own conditions.

The conditions faced by Aboriginal reserves in Canada are often compared with those of marginalized communities in what is called the developing world. Added to this is the burden imposed by very high rates of alcohol abuse and suicide. Similar conditions have been described in white settlements that were established by the Hudson Bay Company in the Canadian north in the 1700 and 1800s. They, too, were rife with alcohol abuse: the result of an oppressive environment. It happens when people are dislocated from their own ways, from the context they know. This leads us to another example of context, this one involving rats and drug addiction.

Rat Park: the context leads to addiction

Rat Park was a study of drug addiction conducted in the 1970s by Canadian psychologist Bruce K. Alexander at Simon Fraser University in British Columbia. Alexander's hypothesis was that drugs do not cause addiction. He found that the apparent addiction to morphine commonly observed in laboratory rats exposed to it is attributable to their living conditions, and not to any addictive property of the drug itself. He told the Canadian Senate in 2001 that experiments in which laboratory rats are kept isolated in cramped metal cages, tethered to self-injection apparatus, show only that 'severely distressed animals, like severely distressed people, will relieve their distress pharmacologically if they can'.

To test his hypothesis, Alexander built Rat Park, a 200-square-foot (18.6 m²) housing colony, two hundred times the square footage of a standard laboratory cage. There were 16–20 rats of both sexes in residence, an abundance of food, balls and wheels for play, and private places for mating and giving birth. The results of the experiment appeared to support his hypothesis. Rats that had been forced to consume morphine hydrochloride for fifty-seven consecutive days were brought to Rat Park and given a choice between plain tap water and water laced with morphine. For the most part, they chose the plain water. 'Nothing that we tried', Alexander wrote, 'produced anything that looked like addiction in rats that were housed in a reasonably normal environment.' The two major scientific research journals, *Science* and *Nature*, rejected Alexander's paper, which appeared instead in *Pharmacology Biochemistry and Behaviour*, a respectable but much smaller journal, and the paper's publication attracted no response. Because of the lukewarm reception, Simon Fraser University withdrew Rat Park's funding (Wikipedia, n.d.).

Since the article was published (Alexander et al., 1981) Bruce Alexander has continued to examine how context affects human addiction. His work focuses on dislocation as a precursor to addiction (Alexander, 2001). Whether the context is that of Aboriginal Canadians, or Scottish immigrants to Canada in the 1700s, when people are dislocated, addictive behaviours emerge. None of the prevention programmes will work until the root causes of social, economic and cultural dislocation are addressed.

'Changing the terms of this debate is a huge task, since the current manner of speaking of addiction as an individual drug-using disease is maintained by a media army that has been launching this message for decades' (Alexander, 2001: 19). Alexander is not alone: the case of campaigns against cocaine abuse in Europe fall into the same trap. The focus is on slogans that seek to change behaviour without addressing the root causes (Portela Freire, 2007). The focus on public relations has been more attractive than the seemingly behind-the-scenes efforts in education and engagement. The planners like the public-relations approach: it is showy with mass-media slogans and billboards. The searchers, on the other hand, first listen to the context; though the efforts in education and engagement are not so visible. This is the case of the Femina HIP example in the previous chapter.

HIV/AIDS communication recognizes context

The HIV/AIDS pandemic has certainly put Communication for Development in the limelight. Major global investments have gone into combating the spread of the disease, especially in Africa, with attention now also on India and China. Much of the early work focused on individual and behaviour change. These efforts mostly failed because they were based on a series of mistaken assumptions. The early approaches assumed that information alone would lead to behaviour change. They also assumed individuals are able to control their context, when in fact the most vulnerable cannot. They assumed individuals to be on a level playing field when in fact those in the lower socio-economic segments are the most vulnerable. They assumed that individual women can make decisions of their own free will about condom use, when in fact it is largely men who determine what protection is used. Finally they assumed individuals make decisions in a rational manner, when in fact sexual behaviour is more complex (Singhal, 2003).

The case of the Sugar Daddies in Kenya, where young school-age girls are lured into having sex in exchange for cash, cell phones and car rides has been well documented. Girls are well aware of the risks but have a hard time resisting the glamour. The wealthy men, on the other hand, increase their sense of virility when bedding young women. In this context messages about abstention will fall on deaf ears (Singhal, 2003). Today the trend is shifting away from individual level theories, and onto cultural ones that embed themselves in context.

We saw how the Femina HIP media in Tanzania focuses on context. That project helps real people tell their own stories to ensure that a sense of reality comes through. The fact that Minou Fuglesang is trained as an anthropologist no doubt gave credence to this approach. In fact, Femina HIP works very much in line with the approach for HIV/AIDS prevention developed by South Africa's well-known Soul City, a health promotion project. Soul City was started by Garth Japhet, a doctor and part-time journalist who wanted to put the power of the media 'in the service of preventing the spread of HIV and promoting healthier lifestyles' (Gumucio-Dagron, 2001: 176). It produces a television drama series in prime time, radio repeats of the television series, and health education packages. The Soul City approach challenges many aspects of the social environment that lay at the bottom of the AIDS epidemic.

This Femina HIP and Soul City shift where context is rediscovered is based not only on culture but on a human rights approach (Ford et al., 2003). The human rights approach begins by recognizing that the people living with HIV/AIDS deserve to have a voice and speak about their concerns (Tufte, 2005). This resonates with Wilna Quarmyne's emphasis on people having a right to voice their views. The call is for a holistic approach, one where those who live with HIV/AIDS are not seen as a passive audience, but rather as the ones who can understand the context from the inside and identify solutions. One example from Tanzania focuses on street children who produce theatre plays about HIV/AIDS, after receiving some basic training in drama and the biology of the disease (Bagamoyo College of Arts et al., 2002). This shift to recognizing context and work within it gives us hope; it would appear that the planners are giving way to the searchers.

Communication for Development programmes, especially large campaigns in the health sector, take context into account. Yet context is dynamic, it is political and complex, and it can come back to haunt you in unexpected ways. This happened in the case of the Global Polio Eradication Initiative. In the late 1980s the World Health Organization took the lead over the Initiative.

> In 1988, more than a thousand people a day were infected with polio in 125 countries. By 2003, only 784 people worldwide contracted polio *for the entire year*, and polio was endemic in only six countries: India, Pakistan, Afghanistan, Egypt, Niger and, alone responsible for nearly half of the new cases, Nigeria. (Rosenstein and Garrett, 2006: 20)

The numbers are impressive and a testament to the power of a program that embraces communication and is well designed. However, Rosenstein and Garrett also describe how in Nigeria the campaign came to a shocking halt. An emir in a northern state did some searching of his own, gathering materials from the Internet, and concluded that the campaign was a Western conspiracy. He made it known that the vaccine was unsafe and possibly linked to sterilization. The result was that within eighteen months the disease had spread once again to sixteen countries. Following the hajj of February 2004 (when Muslims congregate in Mecca) it spread all the way to Indonesia. The Nigerian context was further complicated by ineffective medical facilities, ethnic and religious fragmentation, and a distrust of outsiders. The context came back to undo what had up until then been a poster child for health communication.

Media policy shapes context

After Independence several government institutions were set up in the city of Ahmedabad, India, in honour of Gandhi's home. This brought Vikram Sarabhi to head the Indian Space Research Organization (ISRO). ISRO in turn started the Satellite Radio Program and was the home of the 1975 Satellite Instructional Television Experiment (SITE), which introduced satellite communication for rural broadcasting. Kiran Karnak and his colleague E.V. Chitnis worked in the government-supported SITE research office at the Space Application Centre (SAC) in Ahmedabad. They decided to stay with government to launch what they describe as an activist media project in the village of Kheda (circa 1978). The District of Kheda was very close to the Space Application Centre headquarters in Ahmedabad. Gujerat owned Kheda the way Calcutta owned Chitrabani.

Wendy talked with Kiran Karnak in New Delhi in February of 2008. Kiran was passionate when he talked about Kheda thirty years later. This was particularly poignant when you consider his subsequent huge success with Indian Telecom, which won him Forbes Man of the Year.

The Kheda project was an experiment within government. It used government media to reach out to the rural areas, encouraging participation at every level.

The Kheda team from SAC consciously chose to focus on the structural problems faced by the rural poor and used television to 'awaken' the audience in the Freirian sense. The programmes attempted to promote self-reliance among the community by showing that change was possible through optimal use of local resources without depending on external agencies....The prime target audience of Kheda Rural Television, according to the programme managers, were the rural poor who needed the 'catalytic input' that would help them to help themselves. (Ghosh, 2006: 53)

The villagers themselves wrote, acted and determined many of the programmes. In this way, issues were raised around caste, exploitation, alcoholism and other taboo subjects. The Kheda project collaborated with extension agencies, local banks and any one else who could help facilitate use of the information that came from the programmes. It was an amazing experiment – a government-led enterprise with full government funding that raised community issues which quite often contravened the status quo.

> We started the experiment during Indira Gandhi's state of emergency. In no time our work was seen as insidious and they tried to shut us down. But, the good thing was that we too were government (INSAT) and we fought back saying that one government body could not shut down another government body. We believed strongly in the necessity of having champions within the government to try to bring change within ... and this worked – they didn't shut us down. Then we got a new government (BJP) and the new government got uneasy. We were called communists, we were accused of instigating unrest, and we were telling women to go out and work and ignore the words of their husbands. They started by trying to shut down the Kheda transmitter. All the villagers surrounded it and wouldn't allow it to be shut down. But the central government was determined and found a way to get around it. They did not use force – they were astute. They said they would broadcast the same thing but from Ahmedabad – they didn't understand the whole point and purpose and necessity of local decentralization – so the program got switched to Ahmedabad and of course it got diluted. After about four years of struggle the whole idea died down. We succeeded for a while and then failed. (Karnak, personal communication)

The Kheda success depended on a more open government policy. When that shifted, the orchid wilted. Government policy on media and communication is so much part of the context that we often forget its powerful impact. In India, for example broadcasting was completely controlled by the government until well into the 1990s. This had a major impact on restricting media potential. It also caused places like Chitrabani to struggle to present an alternative. In the early days when the use of satellite for broadcasting was being planned for SITE, several people argued that SITE could be used to 'give the community back to itself' by using television as a dialogical tool and social mirror. However, it was too late in the planning to make the change (Ghosh, 2006). Finally in 1996 the Indian government acknowledged that the airwaves belonged to the public not to the government or the private sector. The government passed a new Community Radio law in 1996. It has taken a long time to take root.

Context drives functions

We think of context as establishing which of the communication functions may work. Waad El Hadidy, for example, wrote a piece reflecting on the difficulties of working with participatory communication in the Arab world (El Hadidy, 2006). She explained that despite the deep roots of participatory practices within the religion and the culture, the present political environment (history, politics) makes the practice less than viable. This observation clarifies our point that it would not make sense to lead projects with a participatory communication approach, something that has been confirmed by other communication practitioners in the region (Zaid, 2008). Waad reminds us to recognize context. You don't force communication approaches in a context that does not invite it.

In Chapter 6, we recounted how Don Snowden had laid down 'ground rules' before he would accept any work in a different context. They resonate as much today as they did when he spoke twenty-five years ago. They stay in our memory. Like Roberge, he was alive to the power of the visual media. At the same time he was acutely conscious of its potential for putting others into political trouble.

Several times we have been tempted to introduce participatory video in situations that are not ideal. And, yes, there have been times when we have succumbed. It is a personal thing. You get the feeling that if only we could get a chance to 'show' what video can do, the rest will follow. The trouble is, the rest usually doesn't follow. Wendy asked Paul MacLeod to come and work with her in Kabul to introduce the potential for participatory video with the two partner Afghan NGOS involved in her project. Paul is a brilliant trainer who worked side by side with Snowden. Wendy tells how the extension staff clearly loved the possibilities that he opened up for them. Staff went off alone and came back with wonderful material. One of the tapes was a video of a team cleaning a *karaiz* (the ancient Persian irrigation systems prevalent in the south of Afghanistan). It was the first time many had a chance to see this and it spoke volumes about the risk of the business. But who else was going to listen?

Paul MacLeod and Wendy knew they couldn't parachute in with an idea like this and not stick around for a long enough time to see it take root. They had to find a venue to apply the practice. They lobbied with those preparing the Afghan National Development Strategy (Afghanistan's name for what the World Bank calls a Poverty Reduction Strategy), hoping they would be interested in carrying through with the process. There is a mandate for all of these strategies to use methodologies to 'listen to the voice of the poor.' The mandate is there but it is seldom enacted. This reminds us of Father Roberge's emphasis on the difficulty of ensuring that what is voiced is heard. In Kabul there was slight interest but no action – that takes time and the strategy was well down the road towards completion. Inevitably the project on which Wendy worked was over and their efforts had to end. Later, some of the ideas were revived through a different small project around *participatory poverty assessment*, but more as 'show and tell' than a replication of the process. Paul was involved in the later application, and he wrote:

> Of course, the problem there from the beginning was that there were no field staff people in place to do anything with it and so no possibility of any real 'working' of it at any level, let alone using it as a tool for advocacy of any kind. It was a scattered activity without any process. I just hope it didn't hurt anybody.

Listening to the context

Listening to the context is about appraising, learning, recognizing and appreciating all those dimensions so that we can make well-informed decisions. Our development literature is full of examples of appraisal techniques. We find that the challenge is less about the tools, and more about the project context. Projects are artificial and limited by regulations, funding, predetermined objectives and time lines.

The truth is our desire to show potential gets in the way of judgement. So often is it too late when we realize the conditions are not conducive for listening. This happens over and over in the grey zone. We so often work with short projects that walk away. The last example is among them, but it has elements of hope. It helps us build a case in Chapter 9 that there is room to do good communication if you navigate with your eyes open. Focus on the communication functions that fit the context. Like Minou Fuglesang, gradually begin to push the boundaries.

We cannot think of anyone who illustrates the importance of listening better than Mahatma Gandhi. Gandhi demonstrated the power of communication every single day. Ashoke Chatterjee explained this to Wendy when she paid him a visit.

Ashoke emphasized that Gandhi was meticulous in his preparation, careful in his listening and adamant in his follow-up. He determinedly left his people behind in every community he touched to ensure that this would happen. The famous salt march, Ashoke explained, was preceded by two or three years of preparation and listening. Gandhi realized that whatever act he decided to follow must be such that news would spread and the symbolism of the act would be well understood.

He sat in Ahmedabad figuring out what he could do to explain to the people what freedom was all about. He realized that once he picked up a grain of salt he would be put in jail. This, then, is what he decided to do, but he made sure the act was accompanied by as much fanfare and attention as he could muster. And indeed he was put in jail for several years, but by then the fire had ignited.

PART III

What we can do differently

NINE

Training and negotiating in the grey zone

Our central argument is that good development makes good commu-nication. Instead of pushing good communication on decision-makers we really should be promoting another (good) development. This argument presents a paradox. Do we use our skills to affect the development context, or do we sit and wait for good development to arrive at our doorstep and then act? We think the answer is a bit of both.

In this chapter we focus on the choices at hand to improve what we do while working in the grey zone. We use our coordinates (cham-pions, context and functions) and propose touchstones to improve capacity and negotiate more realistic terms of reference to suit the context. We talk about the zone of the possible with suggestions on how to become more selective of champions, challenge short project durations, and find ways to listen to those who live in context. We add another twist: the stage in life. As professionals, the stage in life we are in shapes how we make decisions and what risks we are willing to take. We illustrate how we have used some of the touchstones to navigate in the grey zone.

Training and negotiating

The two aspects of our profession where we still have room to ma-
noeuvre revolve around training people in the field and negotiating the
scope of work. Training is integral to any communication initiative.
On looking back we realize that there has never been a single incident
when we haven't had to build communication capacity as we moved
through the implementation process of any given project.

We have learned that much of success or failure depends on an
ability to negotiate terms before the start. And here we turn to our
coordinates – champions, context and functions – to give us the basis
on which to adjust expectations and the terms of reference. Be it a
short consultancy or a full-time job, the very start is the deciding
moment.

We often think of a British colleague, Simon Bachelor, who negotiated a contract to head an NGO in Cambodia. He had the audacity
to negotiate a full first year of work without having to spend a single
dollar. He used this time to immerse himself in the context. He got
to know the stakeholders and sought out potential champions. We
imagine that people saw him as Simon, not as $imon. By the end of
that year he had a very good idea of where to put his second year's
money; in fact he was itching to have some to spend. No budget as a
communication strategy – just listening.

In this chapter we provide a number of touchstones both in the
training area and in negotiating the scope of work. We call them
touchstones to emphasize that they are not recipes, but markers to
guide our work.

TRAINING TOUCHSTONE 1:
LIKE LEARNING A NEW LANGUAGE

We have always found it necessary to clarify what we mean by communication. And many times we have thought that everybody else
was either obtuse or deliberately not understanding what we meant.
It took us a while to figure out that in some cases people may well
have understood the approach but simply did not want to do it. Those
in power know that participation will bring trouble, so they stick to
safe, one-way communication functions. This may be only part of the

problem. We are beginning to see that developing a 'communication' mindset is like learning a new language – and not all of us are good at teaching language.

In Chapter 4 we talked about 'left-brain' versus 'right-brain' thinking. As a development professional you are taught skills to make you believe you know best (left brain). Now you are told to be more open: 'let's look at this situation and see what we can learn together' (right brain). Making this transition is not easy. Notions of self-esteem, professional identity, social class and prestige have a hold on our brain, so too does our culture. How do we reach that 'flip of a switch' sensation you get when struggling with a new language and suddenly find yourself thinking in it? Ah, you realize, you are seeing the world through a different set of eyes.

The notion that learning communication is like learning a new language comes from the authors of an approach called Social Analysis Systems (www.sas2.net). It is not strictly a communication approach, but it makes a lot of sense to us: it is about understanding context. They began exploring methods for stakeholder analysis. Soon they had a vast collection of methods to engage people in understanding their context. They were meticulous in their organization of the methods and they spent years training facilitators how to use them. They went all over the world testing the idea. Their experience is clear: to learn this technique, you must practise it. It takes time to gain the confidence to adapt and adjust the different methods. You start learning by using SAS in conversation; you realize one day that you are working in a different mode. One of the authors says that learning SAS is not fast food. It is as hard and as rewarding as learning a new language. Wendy remembers an experience that relates to this.

Years ago I was working in the water sector in Pakistan, I remember sitting with a group of water engineers. It must have been the mid-1990s when the whole notion of community demand and payment for water services was high on the international agenda. I can still feel the frustration. I would ask 'if you want the community to pay shouldn't you begin with the community and ask what they want?' At that time the engineers were so used to being in charge of planning, they couldn't flip the switch away from them and over to the community. We are hard-wired to be 'in the know'.

Once we understand that learning to listen, to do good communication, is like learning a new language, we are in a better position to
negotiate how to do this. It is a metaphor that can help us; we are
better able to determine trainee selection, format, methods of learning
in the field, and the time required.

TRAINING TOUCHSTONE 2: CELEBRATING COMMON-SENSE COMMUNICATION

We come into this world with a communication common sense: we
scream when we are born. We are given a language that shapes how
we organize what we see, hear and feel. Along comes our schooling
and the media. Both meddle with our heads: most of us end up
confusing communication with information. McLuhan and Roberge
tell us that the media shape us to the point where we no longer
notice it. If we have a communication common sense and yet at the
same time our media environment is reshaping us, what choices do
we have? How can we regain it and act? What does it take to become
searchers that listen? Here are some examples.

Communication training for future medical doctors in the UK is
based on a careful understanding of context (Brown, 2008). The introduction of neoliberalism by the Thatcher government coincided with
the advent of the Internet. As patients became better informed via the
Internet, their relationships with doctors shifted. The 'expert patient'
was now a 'customer'; there was a rise in litigation against doctors. Jo
Brown explains how these contextual factors, and their effects, shaped
the communication curriculum in UK medical schools. Now a clinical
communication course pays much attention to the patient–doctor
relationship. 'Poor communication and attitudes [are] at the heart of
litigation against doctors' (Brown, 2008: 276). Ricardo related this
story during a meeting of Canadian Veterinarians without Borders
and he learned that veterinarians share these experiences. Not only
that: one of them told him that she would be leaving her job soon
because of the poor communication practices of the lead veterinarian
in her clinic.

In his book *Blink*, Malcom Gladwell reports on how insurance
companies in the United States make decisions to insure doctors on
the basis of the quality of their communication with patients:

The surgeons who had never been sued spent more than 3 minutes longer with each patient that those who had been sued did (18.3 versus 15 minutes)... They were more likely to engage in active listening, saying such things as 'Go on, tell me more about that,' and they were far more likely to laugh and be funny during the visit. Interestingly, there was no difference in the amount of or quality of information they gave their patients; they didn't provide more details about medication or the patient's condition. The difference was entirely in *how* they talked to their patients. (Gladwell, 2005, 41–2)

Beyond doctors and veterinarians, this pattern is also true for non-governmental organizations (NGOs). A review of how British Overseas NGOs perform concluded that 'the quality of an NGO's work is primarily determined by the quality of its relationships with its intended beneficiaries' (Keystone, 2006, vi).

This common sense is increasingly rare in customer services – try to get help from your phone company. Yet some private businesses have known how important it is to acquire and retain customer loyalty. Two decades ago Scandinavian Airlines realized that passengers would make up their minds about how much they liked the airline mainly during check-in. This was a 'moment of truth' when the quality of service made all the difference (Carlzon, 1987). The airline went on to ensure that the staff handling the key moments of truth had as many resources and as much authority as possible. Such moments of truth make a lot of (common) sense.

TRAINING TOUCHSTONE 3: CAN COMMUNICATION FOR DEVELOPMENT BE LEARNED AT UNIVERSITY?

Yes it can, but not from books alone. People learn a great deal more if they come to the communication field with some practical experience. Ricardo witnessed this when he taught graduate courses in a university programme on Capacity Development and Extension. Those who had worked in rural and international development were best able to connect theories and cases studies with applied projects in the community. They could understand the complexities, the inbuilt contradictions. They had felt the limits of left-brain thinking and were hungry for the right side. He combined class teaching with applied community projects, creating an apprenticeship programme that worked.

Manuel Calvelo Rios, one of the champions we profiled in Chapter 6, insists that most Latin American undergraduate communication programmes produce graduates who are ill suited to rural development. They come out of journalism programmes with an urban and commercial bias. They are no longer able to empathize with rural people. They are trained to tell, not to listen.

Years ago in Cali, Colombia, Ricardo was working for another NGO. One of his tasks was to train agricultural communicators. He put an advert in the newspaper that read something like:

> Wanted: agricultural communicators. Will be trained on the job.
> Candidates to send a draft, incomplete drawing of crops to be
> shown to – and corrected by – farmers.

He received three submissions. The first two he discarded on the spot: they were finished, formal, tidy, urban, glossy presentations. The third, to his great relief, was rough, unfinished, scrappy and perfect. Any farmer would feel comfortable fixing it. The applicant for the job had worked as a community development worker. The other two – an architect and an engineer (professionals desperate for work) – had no understanding of context. Worse, they had not been trained to listen.

There are graduate programmes in Communication for Development in several countries, though not enough of them. The Communication for Social Change Consortium has helped assemble a network of about a dozen universities around the world – a great achievement complemented by a standardized Master's curriculum. There are dozens of other programmes where communication is a component or a field of specialization within a given discipline. We find these to be particularly important, even at the undergraduate level. Ricardo was often disappointed to see engineering students drop out of his undergraduate introductory course to agricultural extension. He could see the benefits that a listening mode would bring to their left-brain career, but they could not. Was it already too late to learn a new language?

The teaching methods have to change. Think of the numerous long and inappropriately elaborate manuals. They seem to exist in a world with no apparent time limit; we usually cast them aside. We are convinced that it is those who actually produce the manuals who learn the most. Yet donors love to release them as if they were best-sellers. Donors are also keen to fund workshops; a modality with plenty of challenges. We realize that we are just learning how to teach this language.

TRAINING TOUCHSTONE 4: WORKSHOP WORSHIP

Fairly recently we prepared a week-long training plan to introduce communication for development to a large group of government agricultural officers from countries in the Middle East. We were worried about this because we needed to pack a lot of information into a short time frame. We set our agenda and work plan. We sent it to the organizers and we prepared our handout material. So great was our desire to cover the groundwork that we failed the first and most crucial step. We did not devote the first session to listening and trying to understand the type of communication support each person felt was needed specific to his/her particular work. It was quite a week.

At the end of the workshop the organizer asked us what we thought about holding a follow-up workshop in another venue. No, we said; we didn't think that another workshop would make sense. It had become very clear to us that it would be much better to select one or two countries and provide mentoring to a few officers as they applied communication thinking and methodologies to their actual work. Our conclusion: you would not learn a language from a book; what was clear was the need for a more experiential type of learning.

Earlier, Guy Bessette from the International Development Research Centre (IDRC) had warned us that you can't do this in a one-week workshop setting. And of course he was right. Guy had been quietly spearheading Igsang Bagsak, an experiential learning programme in Southeast Asia and Southern Africa and knew that learning needed to take place over an extended period and through 'on the ground' experiences. They were selective of researchers who had an interest in learning about communication. The emphasis was on appropriation and ownership over the research; support for local initiatives; sharing of knowledge and building of partnerships. Lastly, it focused energy on influencing policymaking (Bessette, 2006).

Over the last two years we have run several other workshops and consultancies with more success. Participants were selected though a competitive process to lure out the keener, the future champions. We dedicated time to listening to what they understood, had achieved and wanted to learn about 'communication'. We made an effort to understand the context, especially the organizational culture. In all cases, the trainees were the protagonists of follow-up design and implementation – they were the ones in context. If they were champions, all the better. We limited our role to coaching, not designing. We listened more and planned less; we searched more and told less.

The IDRC approach illustrates our training touchstones. The trainees were given the opportunity to grow within their working context. They gradually explored new ways of thinking and began speaking 'the new language'. The workshops were part of a larger whole. A great deal of online networking was made possible, but only once a community of practice has been created by face-to-face dialogue. This may be the ideal to strive for, one that may be outside the grey zone.

Negotiating the zone of the possible

The second dimension where we have some control is the negotiation of the scope of our work. Here we lean on our coordinates to guide a negotiation.

While many of us may not get the chance to be as successful as our friend Simon, we do for the most part have the chance to negotiate our terms of reference prior to taking on an assignment. This may turn out to be the one moment where we do get to control some of the variables. This may be a luxury depending on your stage in life – more on this later. Consider these proposals:

NEGOTIATION TOUCHSTONE 1: LURING THE CHAMPIONS OUT OF THE WOODWORK

Champions tend to be born not made. There is no particular identification mark to show that someone is going to be a champion;

nevertheless there are some things that can be done to find champions.

Don Snowden would not take on an assignment until he had found the right person or organization to work with and stay behind to carry on with the results. When Ricardo worked on a project in Central America he suggested that the partner teams be found through a competitive process. This gave him a definite leg-up prior to starting the project. He will explain this example later in the chapter. Conversely, participants to the Near East Workshop on communication were selected by governments more for their level of service than for their particular interest in communication.

Competitive processes lure the champions out of the woodwork. During the 1990s, the Canadian government developed the Community Access Program (CAP) to bring the Internet to communities, many of them rural. The modest funding covered the cost of a trainer, a computer and some of the costs of the dial-up connectivity. To become a CAP site, the application had to come from at least two people in the community who worked in the non-profit sector. This requirement meant that a nurse or a teacher who felt the technology had something to offer would need to come together and write the proposal. The process lured champions. In the rating of applications, more points were given to applications that emphasized what the technology would be used for. Only the champions in context were able to figure this out, and the competitive process gave them the opportunity to put their dreams into action. Many of the CAP sites went on to become community-based organizations, all run by champions (Ramírez et al., 2005). Brian Beaton of K-Net, one of the champions described in Chapter 7, made use of the CAP programme, as did numerous other local groups in the country. Insisting on a competitive process to select trainees is a start, especially if it awakens the champion side of young people who have yet to realize their own potential.

NEGOTIATION TOUCHSTONE 2: A COMMUNICATION STRATEGY IN ONE MONTH – NO THANK YOU

We have often been asked to come in and develop a communication strategy. The time given: one month. This really doesn't work. We have learned to suggest that a communication initiative be developed through a phased approach over a longer time frame. This gives us the chance to understand something about the context and gives others the space to allow new ideas to gel. Also, as the context evolves the strategy needs adjustment. Organizations need someone who understands the strategy, who has a sense of ownership over its purpose and design, and who gains a confidence to adjust it as conditions change.

Asking for this is not always easy. In Mozambique it meant that the government had to go to tender because contracts over a stipulated time frame could not be sole-sourced. This also means returning to the country again and again. This adds to the budget, but it is important. We have learned that you cannot develop a communication strategy without taking time to assess the culture of the organization, its ethos, its hierarchy; the nature of the country, its government, its power structure; the relative roles of men and women, tribes and customs; and other communication initiatives that worked or did not. Understanding context feels like doing an organizational audit. It provides the background for moving forward. Without it you are working in a vacuum.

If Communication for Development is like learning a new language, short assignments will yield short-lived benefits. It is much like borrowing an 'Introduction to Arabic' CD and listening to it on the way to work. No classes, no immersion, no learning the new language. Take your time, insist on it, and remind yourself that you are not a champion in context.

NEGOTIATION TOUCHSTONE 3: LEARNING IN CONTEXT

We haven't always been realistic about what is possible in each context and we realize this has cost a lot of time and pain. In Afghanistan a young colleague was disappointed. He tried to bring Afghan deputy ministers to a television studio to record their reaction to videos of community voices. Not one showed up. At a different time, and in Canada, Wendy was a researcher for the popular television programme *Ombudsman*. Once a month a cabinet minister was grilled on air after viewing a story on different issues affecting Canadian life (one of hers was a documentary on the care of the old in Canada). The show went well. The context was completely different.

In Mozambique we tried to match function to context. Our role was to help the government develop a communication strategy to disseminate the National Water Policy. That was all straightforward policy communication. But even this was difficult. Government wanted a strategy common to all provinces. We insisted on a common process of research to be done in each province to adjust the strategy to each context. Try as we might we could not seem to get anyone in the government to understand the need for audience research – for learning in context.

We found that field-testing materials revealed a multitude of ambiguities. The audit aspect became very real. We wrote about this in an article:

> The field-testing in Inhambane revealed a multitude of ambigui-
> ties. For example, there was a lack of clarity around the exact
> amount that a community would be expected to pay for capital
> costs. This ambiguity came into focus when community groups
> were confronted with flash cards generating discussion around
> the issue of payment.... After the field-testing, the Communica-
> tion Team attempted to move forward with full scale publication.
> This proved difficult. Clearly the printing of the materials would
> force the government hand in making those difficult decisions
> on the issue of community contribution and the loss of political
> power ... it was not possible to fudge the issue in the presence of
> a Communication Strategy that sought to clarify procedure and
> promote transparency. (Ramírez and Quarry, 2004b: 11)

Eventually the formulation of the communication strategy brought people back to the table to renew discussion on the National Water Policy. A communication initiative can almost inadvertently be more than it seems. When Ricardo finally went to the field bringing some government officials to participate in the exercise, the actual experience of fieldwork for the research produced a deep understanding that no words could ever convey. We now see we were using a left-brain approach to explain a right-brain function.

In the zone of what is possible we have explored the importance of participant selection. We have found that people learn the most when they are the ones who develop the communication strategy *in situ* and we coach and support. It is experiential learning that works the best, much like a language immersion.

We now add a fourth dimension: the age of the person doing the negotiating and learning. We have come to realize that the stage in life we are in shapes how we make decisions, what risks we are willing to take, and how hard we are able to negotiate in the grey zone.

NEGOTIATION TOUCHSTONE 4: STAGES IN LIFE

It is one thing for Don Snowden, as he was, a man in his fifties and well established in his field, to turn down projects if he didn't feel the conditions were right. It is quite another for someone trying to get started in the field. We realize that. We've been there.

We have thought about this generational twist over the years. We notice, for example, that both Easterly and Collier wrote their books *after* a long career at the World Bank and when they were settled in university posts to pay the bills. We imagine them both established enough in their careers to risk the rebuff that criticism will engender.

It is not easy to go out on a limb and criticize the establishment. There are definite preconditions that must exist unless you are one of the rare people (and they do certainly exist) who manage to do this despite the consequences. Most of us are not like this – most of us still have to work (still want to work) and find it difficult to confront what is put on offer. Silvio Waisbord said he is a communitarian by belief but a diffusionist by necessity (Waisbord, 2007). He believes in the participatory function of communication, but his work calls for the dissemination functions. He is not alone.

Father Roberge is aware of another type of dilemma. Wendy asked him whether he felt that he had been protected by working with the Jesuits. 'Oh yes', he answered immediately; 'this is one of those contradictions. The Jesuits ask us to take a vow of poverty and to help the poor yet our order protects us from ever experiencing one of the most potent realities for the poor – that sense of insecurity.'

When Ricardo was on the farm in Colombia he was 23, at a stage in life when he had no fears and activism was a small sacrifice. He was able to listen. He was willing and able to learn from the people he sought to help. He lived like they did. He worked for an organization that embodied these ideas. He was able to try out new ideas that fitted those core principles. In his case this meant working with farmers, making drawings to document what they had jointly learned. They would laugh at his sketches and correct them. He would go along. You can see how much of an impact Andreas Fuglesang's work had on him. He says he was doing Communication for Development without knowing it. This common sense – this language – turned out to have a name. It was a perfect way to learn a new language. His activist days, however, were few. He then migrated to the grey zone. We both did; we thought that working within could be an activist role.

Now you will be wondering how to actually juggle these touchstones. We use them when they seem appropriate to a given situation; we do not think of them as a checklist. Ricardo illustrates this through one such experience where listening to the context was possible.

Listening to the context: a promising example from Central America

In Central America, approximately 14 per cent of all children born are never registered. This negligence by their parents comes back to haunt the children when they want to enrol in Grade 6 or get medical help, let alone find a job or vote. The problem is more acute in rural communities and worst among Aboriginal groups, where unregistered births can reach 40 per cent of the total. The Interamerican Development Bank has been working with governments in the region to reduce this problem of under-registration.

In 2007 Elena Altieri, who was a communication officer within the Bank, decided to test the power of communication. She wanted to taste strategies with a participatory flavour. She was keen to test-drive a manual on 'participatory rural communication appraisal' (Anyaegbunam et al., 2004). I was contracted to spearhead the experiment.

Ten months later, in select communities of Nicaragua, Sislani – an NGO based in Estelí – reported a 33 per cent increase in annual birth registrations relative to 2006. Like you, we were unsure as to what to make of these numbers – bear with me while I explain the next part of the project.

The short-term effects of communication campaigns in health and family planning range from a 3 per cent to a 12 per cent

change. This percentage refers to the number of people who actually change their behaviour relative to the overall population. In
some cases, rates as high as 30 per cent have been achieved in some
immunization campaigns, but these are not average experiences. In
contrast to behaviour change, the reach of the media can touch 40
per cent of the population and beyond (Snyder, 2003). The contrast
between an elevated number of people reached by a medium and a
smaller number of those who change what they do confirms what
we know from social psychology. Being exposed to information is
not synonymous with changing behaviour. This turns out not to be
surprising when you consider that the essential steps of persuasion
and attitude change are: 'attention → comprehension → interpre-
tation → confirmation → acceptance → retention (→ behaviour
change)' (Rohrmann, 2000: 8). Not only are there many steps in
between; many other factors beyond the reach of a communication
intervention influence whether people move from one step to the
next, or lose interest.

In April 2007, Elena and I spent a short time in Honduras with
Comunica, and in Nicaragua with Sislani. Both are small organizations with a track record in community development, media and
advocacy. More importantly, both had competed through a tender
for this job – luring the champions – and had been selected by
the bank to carry out a pilot project in each country. Both projects
were less than a year in duration and had the goal of increasing the
number of children that are registered at birth. Both projects would
develop a participatory communication strategy and measure its
impact.

My job was to help the local organizations with methodology and
evaluation. Unsure about how to navigate I went back to the basics.
I knew that Elena needed to show her peers in Washington that
this worked. She would need to show evidence. The meaning of
'what worked' needed to be made explicit and realistic. At the same
time our Central American colleagues needed to improve on their
established experiences and reputations. My sense was to focus on
collecting data only about those things that we could change.

We decided to do research on three topics. First, understand the
reasons why people did not register their newborns; this would illuminate historical, educational, cultural, institutional and geographic

dimensions of the context. Second, find out who they trusted and what media channels they already used; this would make visible their networks of trust and sources of information, including media preferences. Third, document how much they already knew about the benefits and about the paperwork involved; this would confirm their current knowledge about the procedures in the institutions.

We tried out 'problem trees' – a technique that helps differentiate the causes from the effects of a problem – in this case, birth under-registration. We learned that distance to the registration office was a barrier, as was the cost of having photos taken. We also found out that there was lack of knowledge about the different procedures. People were not clear about who was allowed to initiate the paper-work and with what documentation. In some cases, a lack of trust of the government was also at the root of this apparent negligence. When we looked back at the history of human rights abuses in this region, this did not come as a surprise, especially among Aboriginal groups. The problem tree also pointed at structural barriers; issues that a communication project could not change on its own. We also traced how people perceived the advantages to registration. On this basis we knew what information gaps we had to concentrate on, and that we had to contribute to some form of concientization on the matter.

The second item was to find out what networks of trust were already in place. Who in the community were known to be the natural distributors of information? Gladwell emphasizes that some champions are natural distributors of information. In both countries we learned that it was the teachers, nurses, some committed majors and the midwives who did this on a regular basis. They were trusted. We also looked into the media that were already in use for networking: interpersonal communication, radio and popular theatre were the favourites.

The Comunica and Sislani teams tracked the before and after levels of knowledge about the advantages and the procedures. They developed problem trees at the local level both at the start and at the end of the communication strategy. They drew maps showing the networks of trust, also at the start and at the end. They learned what medium was already popular and worked with it and traced its reach.

Once we set this in motion, Elena and I watched as the Central American tradition of working with – instead of for – community, kicked into gear. In both countries Comunica and Sislani covered the appraisal and planning work with the audiences, with the champions, and with the media representatives. They formed committees at the municipal level to comment, monitor and improve the planning matrices. The creative use of local tradition was astounding: Sislani worked with a muralist who trained children to design and paint the school wall with images and slogans about registration. Comunica employed a national radio host that managed phone-in competitions following the radio dramas.

The Sislani numbers are now up for scrutiny. A 33 per cent change in birth registrations is very significant when we consider the additional barriers that we exposed using the problem tree. Sislani reported impressive changes in knowledge levels about benefits and procedures. The reach of the radio programmes was also very high. What is less clear, as with short-lived campaigns, is how sustainable these changes will be. Beyond that we wonder what elements of this experience may travel elsewhere.

Sislani and Comunica both worked among and with the protagonists of the context. They engaged the workers of both government registration bureaucracies. Local buy-in and ownership were key. In Nicaragua, the least impressive results among the three project sites belonged to the community where the municipal government demonstrated least interest.

It is early days to understand the consequences of these experimental projects. At the time of writing the orchid had fallen off the stem. Elena is no longer at the Bank and there is no funding for a long-term impact study. Up until this time, the Bank's communication approach had been to develop a national, urban-designed, promotional campaign. This alternative is community-based and participatory. If you boil it down, it is simple. If you look back at the touchstones, we did lean on many of them. It is about listening to the context with the protagonists who live in it. It is about using methods and media that work for them. This is not a very radical approach if you think of Another Development.

In this chapter we have provided touchstones to navigate in the grey zone. At times, however, we wonder if we are mostly rearranging deckchairs on the *Titanic*. It has been a relief to realize that all our efforts to inject communication into development programmes cannot significantly change the long-term development agenda. The overall context must first change. For years we berated ourselves over our inability to make ourselves heard: maybe we needed more evidence; maybe we needed to show some cost–benefit analysis; maybe we needed to explain it better. We now believe no matter what we did nor how hard we tried, the planners and decision-makers would not be moved. They are marching to their own agenda for their own reasons – a group of communicators with communication initiatives will not make the difference. But this does not let us off the hook. What it does, we think, is help us be more strategic.

On looking back we feel that, had we fully understood this earlier, we would not have plunged into so many failed efforts working in the grey zone. We would have assessed the situation differently. Instead of hoping against hope that demonstrating a smorgasbord of clever communication initiatives would win people over, we would have narrowed our expectations and gone for quality within the zone of the possible. We should now relocate our efforts away from the grey zone towards working more closely with champions in context. This is not so simple in today's turbulent context.

TEN

Searching and listening: good communication, good development

We began writing this book with the view that an infusion of good communication would result in good development. We knew that it was not possible to have good development without some say from the people for whom it is intended. As we examined our experiences and those of the champions it became clear that communication on its own has not resulted in good development. Exceptions exist and we celebrate them: our orchids. However, in the development industry there is a particular mindset that erodes such achievement. It demands a way of doing business that relies on prediction and order. Yes there can be tinkering around the bottom and moments when some 'people-centred' action can happen, but orchids are few. On the whole the industry has problems with risk and uncertainty; no wonder it prefers the 'telling' communication.

The champions described in this book stay in context for a long time, they pursue the principles of Another Development, and they embrace 'listening' communication. They create organizations that outlive short-term projects. They also access funding from large agencies: Swedish Aid is supporting Minou Fuglesang; UNESCO supported community radio and so did FAO. They cultivate relationships with champions inside the bureaucracies who protect them from the straitjackets of the industry. If they are lucky.

Thinking about this reminds us of Leslie Knott and her experiences as a practitioner. Her stories of working in and out of the grey zone illustrate the challenges facing our profession. We work in a world of contradictions.

In and out of the grey zone

We introduced you to Leslie Knott at the beginning of the book. Her recent work in Afghanistan illustrates how media can be used to listen, to give people a voice. However, there is more to this story.

Leslie travelled by car with a video team stopping in Herat, Badakshan and Jalalabad. They worked through NGOs known in the area, often staying in homes of people in the villages. Leslie would go out and announce that any women interested in learning how to take pictures could meet her at the house the next morning. Of course, Leslie pointed out, the house where she stayed was owned by the wealthiest of the village. This prevented some women from feeling able to come to the training. But many were eager. She organized small workshops to train the women on basics of digital photography. She then handed over cameras for the women to experiment. The next day the women brought the cameras back to the house. Leslie downloaded their pictures onto her laptop and the women selected their five favourites. Sometimes this process was chaotic: in Jalalabad women were climbing all over each other to get a better glimpse of the photos. Leslie then asked each person to tell a story about the picture and she would write it down. When she left she asked each woman for permission to show the pictures in public. Back in Kabul she made prints. The funding agency selected those they wanted for their exhibition.

Back in London Leslie wanted the pictures to be seen. And she succeeded. They came out in the British paper *The Independent*. We saw the online edition; they conveyed the harsh reality of Afghanistan in a vivid manner. This was Communication for Another Development at work; an inspiring example of working out of the grey zone.

Contrast this to the work she did for a multilateral organization also working in Afghanistan. The organization wanted photographs for a brochure and some text to highlight the success of their work. Once again Leslie travelled the country taking pictures of various projects, tramping through villages and sitting on the floor of small houses talking with people – the beneficiaries of the projects. She was given little guidance for the text. When she finished her work, the organization did not approve. They were not happy because people had not been positive enough about the results. She was accused of writing like a critical NGO activist seeking to highlight the negative. Her reaction: 'What could I do? This is what people said.' She toned it down and tried again; such is the work in the grey zone.

Her experience is very common; it resonates with stories we hear from other colleagues. The development industry says one thing and does another. The few development agencies that still have communication on their nameplate are either part of information technology departments, publications and outreach, or public relations. FAO actually shut down its communication unit only months after it co-hosted the first World Congress on Communication for Development. The few colleagues we have in communication units inside multilateral organizations dedicate much of their effort to advocating for participatory communication. They face an uphill struggle against the prevailing support for the 'telling' kind of communication.

The disagreements that take place within the development industry are echoed by what is happening elsewhere. We describe two contrasting examples where there is a heightened interest in the subject. The first one has to do with the term 'strategic communication', which can be heard everywhere these days – boardrooms, political offices and the top command of the military. This example centres on the 'telling' kind of communication; behaviour change and public relations. It is especially popular among the military. The second is totally different and focuses on the power of social media.

Non-kinetic activity

The military has a term specifically for development. They call it non-kinetic activity. Kinetic activity is bombs and guns. Non-kinetic activity is bridge-building, roads, dams, tube wells – and communication. It makes us wonder: how can any form of communication counteract the most powerful message there is – soldiers with guns, bombs and search warrants?

The military thinks it can. The International Security Assistance Force (ISAF) in Afghanistan is particular about its communication strategy. Wendy met a communication consultant in Ottawa fresh from his work in Afghanistan. He noted that ISAF views the current insurgency as a communication war. So do the Taliban, who are increasingly using the Internet to further their goals.

When Wendy moved back to Canada from Afghanistan in 2006 she was expecting to return to work with the Afghan government to develop and manage a communication strategy for the National Solidarity Programme (NSP). Like so many of these possibilities, the intended contract melted away. Six months later she found that it was the Canadian military that had insisted on taking the job.

Wendy's interest stemmed from research she had done for a paper on the NSP. She found that while the programme was ostensibly about building civil society – involving the ordinary Afghan citizen in decision-making and community support – the communication strategy itself was pure public relations. It had nuggets of excellent communication work among the NGOs responsible for implementing the goals of the programme. She had been hoping to help revive these initiatives and broaden the communication to include all those ordinary people who participated in the NSP. Did the army intend to do that?

Later in Ottawa, Wendy met the soldier who had flown into Kabul for three weeks to write the NSP communication strategy. Wendy described the conversation as something akin to two people walking down parallel paths that would never connect. It took her a while to understand that it was the original intent that mattered. The military wanted to make sure the message about the NSP was *getting out* and Wendy had hoped to see the ideas of the people *getting in*.

Social media, a sense of hope

In the last decade we have been surrounded by the hype of the information era. Many of us have become dependent on new technologies. Mobile phones especially are helping the poor (Kenny, 2002). Farmers are getting better prices for their crops, fishers are tracking weather, and remittance workers are sending money home. We are all using the technologies in similar ways to reduce our transaction costs, to keep in touch with loved ones, to pass on news.

Mobile phones are the most powerful and affordable communication technology, reaching the largest numbers of people in history. The press, radio and television reach massive numbers of people, but all of those audiences are passive. With mobiles, people become senders and receivers. Huge numbers of people choose what to say, when and to whom. Never before has this happened on this scale. We have a hunch that this technology will bring more change and promise than years of communication projects. And it is mainly driven by the private sector, not by fickle donors. National regulators have the power to make rural access a condition for licensing; the expansion beyond urban centres is happening.

The combination of community radio and mobile phones phones allows people to connect into the station and have a voice. We have seen this practice take off in rural Africa. When Ricardo was in Uganda he heard of a district politician who regularly joined a call-in radio show and responded to citizens' concerns. He was widely popular. Radio stations that also connect to the Internet select and translate information for vast numbers of listeners. While the poverty-reduction potential of the Internet has been less evident than radio or mobile phones, its potential is complementary.

In *Smart Mobs* (2002) Rheingold explains how people are mobilizing in ways that were unthinkable twenty-five years ago. Social movements are rising on the basis of text messaging; governments have fallen as a result. Rheingold warns that smart mobs can also go wrong. Witness the use of the Internet by terrorist organizations. However, there is still much promise. The combination of mobile phones and the Internet is expanding a *network* way of doing things, one that is defining a new human experience (Castells et al., 2007). The power of these media is beginning to show potential. Corporations and governments are feeling the fire under their feet. The development industry has also realized its potential to improve democracy and accountability.

A colleague was an observer at the 2008 Pakistan elections. He told how he found the experience fascinating. He was sent to observe at a rural voting station in the north. The electoral teams were crowded in a small building while expectant crowds heaved outside. The ballots were counted manually, pieces of papers drawn from a box and stacked in piles to tally the numbers. As soon as the count was finished for each candidate, the officiating officer used his mobile phone to text the count to the crowds outside. This way, he explained, there could be no tampering with the results.

Our high hopes regarding mobile telephony and social media stem from their resonance with the principles of Another Development. They respond to immediate needs, they help people develop their own solutions; they save money. We see signs that there is a new wave of champions making this technology relevant in many creative ways. This phenomenon does not depend on a project. It is coming into its own and emerges as a new language among young champions in every corner of the world.

A global paradox

The contrasting examples of the military and the social media are indicative of a global paradox. We closed the century with increasing levels of global wealth and giant leaps in technology, but also with global poverty and inequality at an all-time high (Coronel and Dixit, 2006). Our communication examples simply illuminate this paradox.

We found solace in the ideas from *Another Development*. We got in touch with the Dag Hammarskjöld Foundation. *Another Development* was still very much alive; in 2006 the Foundation published a reflection about it in their journal *Development Dialogue*. They also sent us a copy of their forthcoming book *What Next: Trendlines and Alternatives*. It paints scenarios taking us forward to the year 2035 (Mooney and What Next Group, 2006).

Fiction and analysis combine here to paint a picture of a polarized world. The book portrays an increased control over resources by a handful of corporate giants with the complicity of governments and regulators. Control means privatization of genes and nanotechnology, combined with cornering government funds in the health, food and environment fields. *What Next* reads like a futuristic novel and we shiver every time we read headlines in the press that echo its predictions. Yet it also conveys a message of hope. Civil society, making use of today's new media, is able to organize, mobilize and make change happen. In one scenario, civil society orchestrates the election of a Brazilian activist as a director general of the World Health Organization. From that position he is able to make changes that were impossible in the past.

What Next is both sobering and inspiring. It closes a circle started with *What Now: Another Development.*

Implications for relocating our field

The development industry is based on a predictable planning approach. Bureaucracies are built on this world-view. We know how difficult it is to change large organizations. Numerous ambitious new directors end up frustrated after trying to change the system to no avail. We salute those few champions within the large aid systems who make spaces for others to innovate. However, we do not believe the development industry can change from within. The government structures that support the large agencies are complicit with the status quo. Whatever change comes will be due to pressure from the outside. The pressure may come from civil society pounding at their door or from other factors in the global context. The impact of energy conservation campaigns pales in comparison with the change brought about by high oil prices. Will similar changes happen within the aid industry due to outside turbulence?

It might appear that we are ringing the death knell of our profession, but we do not think this is the case. Rather that heralding its demise we are advocating a relocation. Relocating our efforts means anchoring our work with organizations where participatory communication can thrive. We mean relocating away from development bureaucracies working in the planning mode, to organizations and champions embracing a searching mode. The relocation is already under way. The emerging social networks of young champions are changing the landscape. The challenge is to create a new language with this generation but not lose track of what worked for the champions of the past.

We rediscovered the principles of Another Development and we equate them with good development. Good development means a process that opens up channels for people to talk to one another. It is a process that allows people to do what Andreas Fuglesang hoped for: to decide the direction of their own development and demonstrate solutions found by themselves. We realized that *Another Development* provided the stage for good communication. It follows that *participatory communication shapes the very nature of development, while 'telling' communication simply promotes the desired development outcome.*

Leslie's experience touches a nerve. The voice she gave women through digital photos is urgently needed in the global debate. At the same time, when she gave voice to 'beneficiaries' of the aid industry who were not happy clients, she was damned. Is the context today that polarized? It need not be if donors begin identifying champions and supporting them over the long term. Does this mean that communication professionals have only two choices: to work in the grey zone or become an activist? The answer is a qualified yes. If we think back to the main thread in *What Next* we believe there is a continuum between the grey zone and activism. However, when you work in the grey zone, the odds of changing the context remain small.

In the last chapter we combined our coordinates (champions, context and communication functions) with the principles of Another Development and proposed touchstones to guide our decisions. The touchstones guide our negotiation about what is realistic in any context. But the challenge is broader than that. It comes down to understanding when it is that Communication for Development can affect the context, as opposed to when we best lay low until the context is conducive to our methods and media. We believe the first option is worth pursuing when some of the conditions are right. If we find a champion in context, especially one who pursues the principles of Another Development, then by all means we jump in. When the conditions are not favourable, we either say no – when our stage in life allow us – or we tone down the expectations. We focus on other communication functions and do them well. We do not fool ourselves by expecting to do participatory communication that sticks.

The crucial condition for communication and Another Development comes back to the champions. Their achievements fly in the face of the cynicism surrounding our field. Somehow they have found the courage to apply sound principles and remain outside the grey zone. We know they cannot be replicated. Yet we sense a change in the air with social media. It may turn out to be a platform for many new champions to emerge. The relocation of our field, away from the bureaucracies, and onto a growing number of activists gives us hope.

Cultivating common sense on the farm

The offices of the Fundación Educadora San Nicolás took up part of a schoolhouse in the town of Envigado. The town had been annexed by the growing metropolis of Medellín and was known around the world because the cocaine drug lords had made it their home. My business card read 'agrónomo promotor' and my job was to work with farmers and demonstration farms in different parts of the Departamento de Antioquia. The fad that we chased at the time was 'appropriate technology'. Today it would fall under the 'participatory technology development' family of practices. My co-worker Ignacio Villa and I had been influenced by Canada's Frontier College – a bastion of adult education in the country (Selman et al., 1998). Since 1899 Frontier College had sent volunteer 'labourer-teachers' to bring literacy to logging camps, shipyards and remote mining towns. During the day, labourer-teachers would work side by side with the same workers that became their students in the evening.

In 1983 we bought seven hectares of overgrown bush by the mouth of the San Juan River, just east of the Gulf of Urabá, twelve hours north of Medellín by jeep. This is the land of magical realism, a place much like the village of Macondo in Gabriel García Márquez's celebrated *One Hundred Years of Solitude*, where everything is possible.

As we carved out a farm in the tropics of northern Colombia it made sense to involve *campesinos* as labourer-teachers. We experimented with biodigesters, with mixed cropping, with Africanized bees, with planting with the moon (Ramírez and Villa, 1985). They knew how to survive in the harsh environment, and what did we have to offer?

The ink had barely dried on our agricultural degrees and we had much to unlearn. We merged what we knew about agriculture with their wisdom. As we wound down in the evenings, trying to grab a bit of breeze in our hammocks, a common disagreement would emerge: who had learned more from whom? Only later did I realize how precious this had been.

References

Alexander, B. (2001) *The Roots of Addiction in Free Market Society*. Ottawa: Canadian Centre for Policy Alternatives.

Alexander, B., Beyerstein, B., Hadaway, P., and Coambs, R. (1981) 'Effect of Early and Later Colony Housing on Oral Ingestion of Morphine in Rats', *Pharmacology Biochemistry and Behaviour* 15: 571–6.

Anyaegbunam, C., Mefalopulos, P., and Moetsabi, T. (2004) *Participatory Rural Communication Appraisal: Starting with the People*. Rome: SADC Centre for Communication for Development and FAO.

Archer, D. (2007) 'Seeds of Success are Seeds for Potential Failure: Learning from the Evolution of Reflect', in K. Buck, and J. Pettit, eds, *Springs of Participation: Creating and Evolving Methods for Participatory Development*, pp. 15–28. Rugby: Practical Action Publishing.

Bagamoyo College of Arts, Tanzania Theatre Centre, Mabala, R., and Allen, K. (2002) 'Participatory Action Research on HIV/AIDS through a Popular Theatre Approach in Tanzania', *Evaluation and Program Planning* 25: 333–9.

Bekalo, I., Rianga, A., Kibue Ogega, Y., Obare, L., and Kariuki, G. (2002) 'Part 1. Stores. Kenya', in C. Lightfoot, C. Alders, and F. Dolberg, eds, *Linking Local Learners: Negotiating New Development Relationships Between Village, District and Nation*, pp. 66–73. Greve, Denmark, and Amersfoort, the Netherlands: AgroForum and ISG.

Berger, P.L., and Neuhaus, R. (1977) *To Empower People: The Role of Mediating Structures in Public Policy*. Washington DC: American Enterprise Institute for Public Policy Research.

REFERENCES 145

Bessette, G. (2004) *Involving the Community: A Guide to Participatory Development Communication*. Penang and Ottawa: Souhbound and IDRC.

Bessette, G. (2006) *People, Land, and Water*. Ottawa and London: IDRC and Earthscan.

Bolte Taylor, J. (2008) *My Stroke of Insight: A Brain Scientist's Personal Journey*. New York: Penguin.

Brown, J. (2008) 'How Clinical Communication has become a Core Part of Medical Education in the UK', *Medical Education* 42(3): 271–8.

Carlson, C. (1999) 'Let's Reinvent "Mediating Institutions"', *National Civic Review* 88(3): 207–9.

Carlzon, J. (1987) *Moments of Truth*. New York: Ballinger.

Castells, M., Fernández-Ardevol, M., Linchuan Qui, J., and Sey, A. (2007) *Mobile Communication and Society: A Global Perspective*. Cambridge MA and London: MIT Press.

Chambers, R. (1997) *Whose Reality Counts? Putting the First Last*. London: IT Publications.

Chambers, R. (2005) *Ideas for Development*. London: Earthscan.

Christmas, J. (2007) *What the Psychic Told the Pilgrim*. Vancouver: Greystone Books.

Collier, P. (2007) *The Bottom Billion: Why the Poorest Countries Are Failing and What Can Be Done About It*. Oxford and New York: Oxford University Press.

Communication Initiative (2003) 'The Drum Beat 200 – Voices on Communication and Change'. www.comminit.com/en/drum_beat_200.html, 31/1/09.

Coronel, S., and Dixit, K. (2006) 'The Development Debate Thirty Years after What Now', *Development Dialogue* 47(1), June: 13–28.

Dag Hammarskjöld Foundation (1975) *What Now? Another Development*. Development Dialogue 1975: 1/2. Uppsala, Sweden: Dag Hammarskjöld Foundation.

De Jager, A. (2006) 'Participatory Technology, Policy and Institutional Development to Address Soil Fertility Degradation in Africa', *Land Use Policy* 22: 57–66.

Díaz Bordenave, J. (1977) *Communication and Rural Development*. Paris: UNESCO.

Dunn, A., Foot, J.. Gaventa, J., and Zipfel, T. (2007) *Champions of Participation: Engaging Citizens in Local Governance*, International Learning Event Report, 31 May–4 June. Brighton: IDS.

Easterly, W.R. (2002) 'The Cartel of Good Intentions: The Problem of Bureaucracy in Foreign Aid', *Policy Reform* 5(4): 223–50.

Easterly, W. (2006) *The White Mans' Burden: Why the West's Efforts to Aid the Rest Have Done So Much Ill and So Little Good*. New York: Penguin.

Edwards, B. (1979) *Drawing on the Right Side of the Brain*. Los Angeles: J.P. Tarcher.

El Hadidy, W. (2006) 'Reflection on Participatory Development and Related Capacity-building Needs in Egypt and the Arab Region', in G. Bessette, ed., *People, Land, and Water: Participatory Development Communication for Natural Resource Management*, pp. 240–48. London and Ottawa: Earthscan and IDRC.

FAO (1987) *A Rural Communication System for Development in Mexico's Tropical Wetlands*. Rome: FAO.

FAO (1991) *Sharing Knowledge: Communication for Sustainable Development*. Video, Development Support Communication Branch, FAO.

FAO (1994) *Communication: A Key to Human Development*. Rome: Communication for Development Service, FAO.

FAO (1995) *Understanding Farmers' Communication Networks: An Experience from the Philippines*. Rome: FAO.

FAO (1996) *Communication for Rural Development in Mexico: In Good Times and in Bad*. Development Communication Case Study 15. Rome: FAO.

Ford, N., Odallo, D., and Chorlton, R. (2003) 'Communication from a Human Rights Perspective: Responding to the HIV/AIDS Pandemic in Eastern and Southern Africa', *Journal of Health Communication* 8: 599–612.

Fraser, C. (1987) *Un Nuevo Enfoque para la Comunicación Rural: La Experiencia Peruana en Video para la Capacitación Campesina*, Estudio de Caso de Comunicación para el Desarrollo. Rome: FAO.

Fraser, C., and Restrepo-Estrada, S. (1998) *Communicating for Development: Human Change for Survival*. London and New York: I.B. Tauris.

Freire, P. (1973) *Education: The Practice of Freedom*. London: Writers & Readers.

Fuglesang, A. (1982) *About Understanding: Ideas and Observations on Cross-Cultural Communication*. Uppsala: Dag Hammarskjöld Foundation.

Fuglesang, M. (1997) 'Lessons for Life: Past and Present Modes of Sexuality Education in Tanzanian Society', *Social Science and Medicine* 44(8): 1245–54.

Ghosh, A. (2006) *Communication Technology and Human Development*. New Delhi: Sage Publications.

Gladwell, M. (2005) *Blink: The Power of Thinking without Thinking*. London: Allen Lane.

Gómez, R., and Casadiego, B. (2002) *Letter to Aunt Ofelia: Seven Proposals for Human Development Using New Information and Communication Technologies*. Ottawa: IDRC Pan America, Raíces Mágicas, ITDG.

Gossé, K. (2006) 'Unspeakable Words Remain Unspoken'. *Glocal Times* 6, April.

GreenCom (2004) *Going to SCALE: System-wide Collaborative Action for Livelihoods and the Environment*. Washington DC: AED.

Gularte Cosenza, E., Ozaeta Calderón, C., and Díaz Salazar, G. (2008) *Otra Comunicación para Otro Desarrollo*. Guatemala: Centro de Comunicación para el Desarrollo, CECODE.

Gumucio-Dagron, A. (2001) *Making Waves*. Washington DC: Rockefeller Foundation.

Gumucio-Dagron, A., and Tufte, T. (2006) *Communication for Social Change Anthology: Historical and Contemporary Readings*. New Jersey: Communication for Social Change Consortium.

Gwyn, S. (1972) 'Cinema as Catalyst', *Film, Video-tape and Social Change Workshop*. St John's, Newfoundland, 13–24 March.

Hamelink, C. (2002) 'Social Development, Information and Knowledge: Whatever Happened to Communication?', *Development, Journal of the Society for International Development* 45(4): 5–9.

Harr, J. (2009) 'Lives of the Saints', *New Yorker* 84(43): 46–59.

Heath, C., and Heath, D. (2007) *Made to Stick: Why Some Ideas Survive and Others Die*. New York and London: Random House.

Henny, L. (1983) 'Video and the Community', in P. Dowrick, and S. Biggs, eds, *Using Video: Psychological and Social Applications*, pp. 167–77. Chichester: John Wiley.

Iglauer, E. (1984a) 'Donald Snowden', *Inuktitut Magazine*: 5–62.

Iglauer, E. (1984b) 'Donald Snowden', *Interaction* 2(3): 5–10.

K-Net (1999) 'Harnessing Communication Technologies: Building Community Controlled Telecommunication Services in Keewaytinook Okimakanak First Nations', Sioux Lookout ON: K-Net. http://smart.knet.ca/archive/fsworkshop/index.html.

Kenny, C. (2002) 'Information and Communication Technologies for Direct Poverty Alleviation: Costs and Benefits'. *Development Policy Review* 20(2): 141–57.

Keystone. (2006) *A Report by Keystone and Accountability for the British Overseas NGO for Development (BOND)*. London: BOND.

Kotler, P., and Roberto, E.L. (1989) *Social Marketing: Strategies for Changing Public Behavior*. New York: Free Press.

Lerner, D. (1958) *The Passing of Traditional Society: Modernizing the Middle East*. New York: Free Press.

Lewis, P. (1977) 'Video in Non-formal Education', *Education Broadcasting International* 64–7, June.

Lightfoot, C., Alders, C., and Dolberg, F. (2001) *Linking Local Learners: Negotiating New Development Relationships between Village, District and Nation*. Greve and Amersfoort: AgroForum and ISG.

Lindquist, E. (2001) 'Discerning Policy Influence: Framework for a Strategic Evaluation of IDRC-Supported Research', Making the Most of Research: Research and the Policy Process, Ottawa: IDRC. www.idrc.ca/en/ev-12177-201-1-DO_TOPIC.html.

Martínez Ruiz, J., Hernández, P., and Ruiz, J. (2006) '¿Hacemos de la comunicación un mercancía?' World Congress of Communication for Development. Rome: The Communication Initiative. FAO, World Bank, 25–27 October.

McAnany, E. (2008) 'Saving the World: A Brief History of Communication for Development and Social Change', paper at IAMCR Congress on Media and Global Divides, Stockholm, 20–25 July.

McKee, N. (1992) *Social Mobilization and Social Marketing in Developing Communities: Lessons for Communicators*. Penang: Southbound.

McLuhan, M. (1965) *Understanding Media: The Extensions of Man*. New York: McGraw-Hill.

McLuhan, M., and Fiore, Q. (1967) *The Medium is the Massage*. New York, London and Toronto: Bantam Books.

Mefalopulos, P. (2008) *Development Communication Sourcebook: Broadening the Boundaries of Communication*. Washington DC: World Bank.

Melkote, S.R. (2002) 'Theories of Development Communication', in W.B, Gudykunst and B. Mody, eds, *Handbook of International and Intercultural Communication*, pp. 419–436. Thousand Oaks, London and New Delhi: Sage.

Mooney, P., and What Next Group (2006) *What Next: Trendlines and Alternatives: The What Next Report 2005–2035*. Uppsala, Sweden: Dag Hammarskjöld Foundation.

Morris, N. (2003) 'A Comparative Analysis of the Diffusion and Participatory Models in Development Communication', *Communication Theory* 13(2), May: 225–48.

Nandago, M. (2007) 'Training and Facilitation: The Propellers of Participatory Methodologies', in K. Buck, and J. Pettit, eds, *Springs of Participation: Creating and Evolving Methods for Participatory Development*, pp. 29–36. Rugby: Practical Action Publishing.

Nederveen Pieterse, J. (2001) *Development Theory: Deconstructions/Reconstructions*. London, Thousand Oaks and New Delhi: Sage.

Nederveen Pieterse, J. (2008) '21st Century Globalization and Development', Media and Global Divides, Stockholm: IAMCR, 20–25 July.

Nemtin, W., and Low, C. (1972) 'Fogo Island Film and Community Development Project'. Film, Video-Tape and Social Change Workshop, St John's, Newfoundland, 13–14 March.

Nishnawbe Aski Nation (n.d.) 'Land, Culture, Community', in Nishnawbe Aski Nation, Thunder Bay, Ontario. www.nan.on.ca.

Patton, M. (2008) *Utilization-Focused Evaluation*. Los Angeles, London, New Delhi and Singapore: Sage.

Portela Freire, M. (2007) 'Record mundial en consumo de cocaína'. *El País*, 31 July.

Quarry, W. (1994) 'The Fogo Process: An Experiment in Participatory Communication', unpublished paper. Guelph ON: University of Guelph.

Quarry, W. (2006) 'Decision Makers DO Want Communication – What They May Not Want is Participation', World Congress on Communication for Development. Rome: Communication Intiative, FAO, World Bank, 25–27 October.

Quarry, W., and Ramírez, R. (2005) 'Analyzing How Decision Makers Perceive Communication for Social Change', *Mazi* 3, May.

Quarry, W., and Ramírez, R. (2008) 'Communication and Common Sense', IAMCR Congress on Media and Global Divides, Stockholm, 20–25 July.

Quebral, N. (2002) *Reflections on Development Communication, 25 Years After.* Los Banos, Philippines: UPLB College of Development Communication.

Ramírez, R., Aitkin, H., Kora, G., and Richardson, D. (2005) 'Community Engagement, Performance Measurement, and Sustainability', *Canadian Journal of Communication* 30(2): 259–79.

Ramírez, R., and Quarry, W. (2004a) *Communication for Development: A Medium for Innovation in Natural Resource Management.* Ottawa and Rome: IDRC and FAO.

Ramírez, R., and Quarry, W. (2004b) 'Communication Strategies in the Age of Decentralisation and Privatisation of Rural Services: Lessons from Two African Experiences', *AgREN Network Paper* 136, July.

Ramírez, R., and Richardson, D. (2005) 'Measuring the Impact of Telecommunication Services on Rural and Remote Communities', *Telecommunications Policy* 29: 297–319.

Ramírez, R., and Villa, I. (1985) 'Where the Campesinos Are Consultants', *CERES* 107, September–October: 34–8.

Resnick, M. (1984) 'Teen Sex: How Girls Decide', *Update Research Briefs* (University of Minnesota) 11(5): 15.

Rheingold, H. (2002) *Smart Mobs: The Next Social Revolution.* Cambridge MA: Basic Books.

Richards, H. (1985) *The Evaluation of Cultural Action: An Evaluative Study of the Parents and Children Program (PPH).* Ottawa: Macmillan and IDRC.

Roberge, G. (2003) 'Development Communication: The Unfolding of Harmony', *MICA Communications Review* 1(1), January.

Rogers, E.M. (1962) *Diffusion of Innovations.* New York: Free Press of Glencoe.

Rohrmann, B. (2000) 'A Psychological Model for Analyzing Risk Communication Processes', *Australasian Journal of Disaster and Trauma Studies*, 2000(2).

Röling, N. (1994) 'Communication Support for Sustainable Natural Resource Management', *IDS Bulletin* 25(2): 125–33.

Rosenstein, S., and Garrett, L. (2006) 'Polio's Return: A WHO-Done-it?', *Contents* 1(3), Spring: 19–27.

Schramm, W. (1964) *Mass Media and National Development: The Role of Information in the Developing Countries.* Stanford CA: Stanford University Press.

Selman, G., Selman, S., Cooke, M., and Dampier, P. (1998) *The Foundations of Adult Education in Canada.* Toronto: Thompson Educational.

Servaes, J and Malikhao, P. (2004) 'Communication and Sustainable Development: Issues and Solutions', paper presented at 9th Communication for Development Roundtable, Rome, 6–9 September.

Sim, R. (1998) *The Farm Forum Story*. Guelph ON. www.uoguelph.ca/~snowden/frf_story.html.

Singhal, A. (2003) 'Focusing on the Forest, Not Just the Trees: Cultural Strategies for Combating AIDS', *MICA Communications Review* 1(1): 21–8.

Snowden, D. (1998) 'Eyes See, Ears Hear', in D. Richardson, and L. Paisley, eds, *The First Mile of Connectivity: Advancing Telecommunications for Rural Development through A Participatory Communication Approach*, pp. 60–73. Rome: FAO.

Snyder, L. (2003) Development Communication Campaigns', in B. Mody, ed., *International and Development Communication: A 21st-century Perspective*, pp. 167–88. Thousand Oaks, London and New Delhi: Sage.

Stuart, S. (1989) 'Access to Media: Placing Video in the Hands of People', *Media Development* 4: 8–11.

Tufte, T. (2005) 'HIV/AIDS Communication: Back in the Trenches?', *The Drumbeat* 297, 2 May. www.comminit.com/drumbeat_297.htm.

Waisbord, S. (2001) 'Family Tree of Theories, Methodologies and Strategies in Development Communication: Convergences and Differences'. www.comminit.com/stsilviocomm/sld-2893.html.

Waisbord, S. (2007) 'The Irony of Communication for Social Change', *Mazi* 12, August. www.communicationforsocialchange.org/mazi-articles.php?id=349.

Waisbord, S. (2008) 'The Institutional Challenges of Participatory Communication in the International Aid System', IAMCR Congress on Media and Global Divides, Stockholm, 20–25 July.

Warren, M. (2007) 'The Digital Vicious Cycle: Links between Social Disadvantage and Digital Exclusion in Rural Areas', *Telecommunications Policy* 31(6–7): 374–88.

White, G. (2007) 'Community Radio in Ghana: The Power of Engagement'. www.c3.ucla.edu/research-reports/reports-archive/editors-perspective/community-radio-in-ghana.

White, S. (1999) *The Art of Facilitating Participation: Releasing the Power of Grassroots Communication*. New Delhi, Thousand Oaks and London: Sage.

White, S., Sadanandan, N., and Ascroft, J. (1994) *Participatory Communication: Working for Change and Development*. New Delhi, Thousand Oaks and London: Sage.

Wikipedia (n.d.) Rat Park. http://en.wikipedia.org/wiki/Rat_Park.

Zaid, M. (2008) 'Implementing a Participatory Communication Approach', IAMCR Congress on Media and Global Divides. Stockholm, 20–25 July.

Index